Transnational Terrorism:
Evolving Threats And Responses

Transnational Terrorism:
Evolving Threats And Responses

Editors

Maj Gen RPS Bhadauria, VSM (Retd), & Dr Roshan Khanijo

(Established 1870)

United Service Institution of India

New Delhi

Vij Books India Pvt Ltd

New Delhi (India)

Published by

Vij Books India Pvt Ltd
(Publishers, Distributors & Importers)
2/19, Ansari Road
Delhi – 110 002
Phones: 91-11-43596460, 91-11-47340674
Mob: 9811094883
e-mail: contact@vijpublishing.com

ISBN: 978-93-90917-88-4 (Hardback)

ISBN: 978-93-90917-89-1 (Hardback)

ISBN: 978-93-90917-94-5 (ebook)

Contents

PART- II

Transnational Terrorism in India's Strategic Neighbourhood

PART- III

Role of Technology & International Security Mechanisms in Countering Transnational Terrorism

PART- IV

Major Takeaways from the Panel Discussion

Foreword

The United Service Institution of India (USI) celebrated its 150th year in 2020. As an autonomous institution with a membership exceeding 15,000, USI provides niche expertise in national security strategy, revolution in military affairs (RMA), trans-border security challenges, international relations, net assessment and strategic gaming, etc. USI has institutional tie up with a number of academic, research and military establishments in India and abroad.

USI regularly conducts International Seminars, Round Table Discussions and Workshops. The annual International Seminar conducted by the USI is highly subscribed by eminent experts from all over the world. The papers presented at the seminars are published in the form of a book. Apropos, the theme of November 2019 Seminar was "Transnational Terrorism: Evolving Threats & Responses". The participants and audience for the seminar were from Think Tanks from across the globe, diplomats from various countries, academicians of national and international repute, professionals from military and various police organisations, government officials, members from the corporate sector and students from various universities pursuing international affairs.

Since, the inception of the National Security Seminar in 2009, the theme of discussion had centered on the geo-strategic opportunities and challenges in the Asia-Pacific and the Indo-Pacific regions. However, with the menace of international terrorism rampantly rising, in 2019 the Seminar's focused shifted to 'Transnational Terrorism', which is also the most - formidable threat in the asymmetric wars of the 21st Century. Transnational terrorists operate simultaneously across continents, and not only challenge the authority of the State, but even threaten their very existence. There seems to be no dearth of volunteers or finances available, to these terrorist organisations.

The Seminar thus, has attempted to address all relevant issues pertaining to transnational terrorism; their ideology, technology, cyber and informative space used as a medium, thereby, giving us an opportunity to identify evolving trends in transnational terrorism and articulate a comprehensive and collective approach to combat it. Further, the seminar had tried to have a cross fertilisation and synthesization of perspectives from various regions, as also identify evolving trends, articulate a comprehensive and collective approach to combat transnational terrorism in all its manifestation, and provide policy inputs to the government agencies and strategic institutions dealing with terrorism.

Maj Gen BK Sharma, AVSM, SM & Bar (Retd)
Director USI

Participants

Shri Kanwal Sibal, IFS (Retd)

Shri Kanwal Sibal, IFS (Retd) is a former Foreign Secretary to the Government of India. He has been Ambassador to Turkey, Egypt, France and Russia. He was a member of India's National Security Advisory Board from 2008 to 2010. He is on the Board of the New York based East-West Institute and member of the Executive Council of the Vivekananda International Foundation. He is an adviser to the U.S.-India Strategic Partnership Forum and Chairman of the Forum of Strategic and Security Studies. He is an Editorial Consultant to the Indian Defence Review and is the Foreign Affairs Editor of 'Force'. In 2011 he was also the President of the Association of Indian Diplomats. He has written more than 500 Op-Eds and other articles on international affairs for major national journals and periodicals. He was awarded *'Grand Officier of the Ordre national du Mérite'* by the French President in 2004. In 2017 he received the *'Padma Shri'* from the President of India. He has been decorated by the Russian Foreign Minister on behalf of the Russian Foreign Ministry for his contributions to international cooperation. His book of poems *"Snowflakes of Time"* has been published in 2016.

Lt Gen P K Singh, PVSM, AVSM (Retd)

Lt Gen PK Singh, PVSM, AVSM (Retd) was commissioned as a Second Lieutenant in the Indian Army in 1967 and retired as Army Commander (GOC-in-C) in 2008. His academic qualifications include M.Sc., MPhil and post-graduate Diploma in Business Management. He took over as Director of the United Service Institution of India (USI) in January 2009 and retired in 2019. He is a member of the Governing Council of the Indian Council of World Affairs, New Delhi, and member of the International Advisory Board of the RUSI International, London. He is also a member of the Advisory Committee of the special centre for National Security Studies, Jawaharlal Nehru University, New Delhi.

Maj Gen BK Sharma, AVSM, SM & Bar (Retd)

Maj Gen Bal Krishan Sharma, AVSM, SM & Bar (Retd), is the Director of USI, at New Delhi. He specialises in Strategic Net Assessments, Scenario Building and Gaming Exercises. He lectures at prestigious military and civil training establishments in India and abroad. He is the editor of USI's '*Strategic Year Book*', and USI's Digital Magazine - '*Strategic Perspective*'. He has also edited books, and authored monographs and occasional papers. He has written articles on strategic affairs, for Indian and foreign journals

Lt Gen Syed Ata Hasnain, PVSM, UYSM, AVSM, SM, VSM & Bar (Retd)

Lt Gen Syed Ata Hasnain, PVSM, UYSM, AVSM, SM, VSM & Bar (Retd) has been involved in various missions, ranging from Sri Lanka to Siachen Glacier, from the North East to Jammu & Kashmir (J&K). He was also involved in the United Nations (UN) operations from Mozambique to Rwanda. He Commanded the Indian Army's Srinagar based 15 Corps and is today one of the foremost writers and analysts on J&K, Pakistan and transnational extremism. He has written articles in many Indian newspapers like, *The Times of India, The Indian Express, The Hindu, DNA, Deccan Chronicle* and *The Asian Age*, besides being a regular participant in mainstream television debates. With a strong academic background from Sherwood College Nainital, St Stephen's College Delhi, the Royal College of Defence Studies and Kings College London, as also the Asia Pacific Centre for Security Studies, Hawaii, he has been at the forefront of encouraging the adoption of the Scholar Warrior concept in the Indian Army. Besides having spoken at the Bangladesh Institute of Strategic Studies (BISS), National Defence College (NDC) and Institute for Policy, Advocacy and Governance (IPAG), (all at Dhaka), he also lectures at the Rajaratnam School of International Studies (RSIS), Institute of South Asian Studies (ISAS), and Lee Kwan Yu School for Public Policy, (all in Singapore). He is also associated with the Vivekananda International Foundation and Centre for Joint Warfare Studies, as Distinguished Fellow and is on the Governing Council of the Institute of Peace and Conflict Studies at New Delhi. He lectures on 'National Security' at various military, civil services and corporate institutions, with a view to enhance India's strategic culture. On 13 Jul 2018, the President of India appointed Lt Gen Hasnain (Retd) as Chancellor of the Central University of Kashmir.

Maj Gen Garba Ayodeji Wahab (Retd)

Maj Gen Garba Ayodeji Wahab (Retd) is the Director General, Nigerian Army Resource Centre (NARC). Before his retirement in the year 2015, he had served the Nigerian Army meritoriously in various capacities. His last three appointments include; Director of Operations at Army Headquarters, General Officer Commanding 1 Division Nigerian Army and the Chief of Administration (Army) at Army Headquarters. He holds a Bachelor of Science Degree in Political Science from the University of Lagos and has two Masters degree in Defence Studies and International Relations both from the prestigious Kings College, London. He is a graduate of Advance Senior Command and Staff Course and the Royal College of Defence Studies, both in the United Kingdom. He is a member of numerous professional and academic bodies including the Harvard Kennedy Business School, Boston, USA. Before his appointment as the DG NARC, he worked as a Security Consultant (Director R&D).

Dr Waiel SH Awwad

Dr. Waiel SH Awwad is a writer and a political analyst. He has been a South Asia based journalist since 1979 and has travelled extensively in most of South and South East Asian countries. He has also been a war reporter covering wars in Sri Lanka, Afghanistan, West Asia, and in the Gulf. He has worked as Bureau Chief of MBC (Middle East Broadcasting Centre), London, MBC-FM Radio, Kuwait, Oman and Damascus Radio. Prior to that, he ran a special program: 'Dateline South Asia' in Arabic, first of its kind with Asian News International (ANI). He has been South Asia Bureau Chief of Alarabiya TV Channel (Dubai Media City). Many of his writings have been published in English and Arabic in major newspapers and magazines. Dr. Waiel, covered wars in South Asia. He was detained in Afghanistan before the fall of the Taliban government and was captured in an ambush during the American invasion of Iraq in 2003, while being embedded with the American Troops. He served as President of the Foreign Correspondents' Club of South Asia (FCC) for two terms 2003-2005 and 2013-2015, and as a President Emeritus for FCC South Asia. He is a recipient of the 5th Rajiv Gandhi Excellence Award 2014 for the best overseas journalist. He is a Fellow at - Ce.S.I. - Centro Studi Internazionali, Italy.

Prof Carol M Burke

Prof Carol Burke has been a Professor at the University of California, Irvine, for the past sixteen years. She began her academic career as an Assistant Professor at the U.S. Naval Academy, where she was promoted to Associate Professor before joining the faculty of Johns Hopkins University. She received her first Fulbright Fellowship to conduct research at both Australia's Tri-Service Academy (ADFA) in Canboro and at the extensive military archives housed at the Australian War Memorial. From 2013-2016, she directed a year-long undergraduate course at her university entitled "War,". In 2015, she received a prestigious 'Mellon Foundation' grant to fund research, exhibitions, graduate and undergraduate courses on the topic "Documenting War." Professor Burke was also a Fulbright Fellow at USI where she was researching on the subject of comparative study of culture and counter-insurgency in the Indian and U.S. armies. In 2008, she was with a combat unit in Iraq and published articles on topics ranging from the dangers faced by local Iraqi interpreters working for American military units, the threats to the few remaining independent journalists in Northern Iraq, to the U.S. Army's controversial Human Terrain System. In 2010-11, she worked for the U.S. Army as a cultural advisor in Afghanistan. She trained a small team and routinely worked 'outside the wire' interacting with locals in contested areas.

Prof Usman A Tar

Prof Usman A Tar (PhD) is Professor of Political Science and Defence Studies, and Director of the Centre for Defence Studies and Documentation, Nigerian Defence Academy. Formerly, he was Associate Research Fellow at John and Elnora Ferguson Centre for Africa Studies (JEFCAS), University of Bradford, UK. Prof Tar is a member of Board of the Social Science Research Council's African Peace Building Network (SSRC/APN) based in New York, USA. He is a consultant for the Westminster Foundation for Democracy (WFD, Nigeria), United Nations Development Programme (UNDP, Nigeria) and Konrad-Adaneur-Stiftung (German Development Fund). He is also a 'Resource Person' to the National Defence College (NDC); National Institute for Policy and Strategic Studies (NIPSS); Armed Forces Command and Staff College (AFCSC); Nigeria Army Resource Center (NARC); Center for Democratic and Practice, Mambayya House, Bayero University Kano; Nigeria Institute for International Affairs (NIIA) and Institute for Peace and Conflict Resolution (IPCR).He has also served as a visiting professor and an external examiner to several institutions of higher learning in Nigeria. Prof Tar was a Member of the Presidential Committee to review the National Defence Policy (NNDP) from November 2014 to May 2015. Currently, he is a member of the Federal Ministry of Defence, a think tank to monitor threats to national defence and security in Nigeria.

Mr Shafqat Munir

Mr Shafqat Munir is currently Head of Bangladesh Centre for Terrorism Research (BCTR) and Research Fellow at the Bangladesh Institute of Peace and Security Studies (BIPSS). In addition to research and analysis on Common Vulnerabilities and Exposures (CVE), he also focuses extensively on strategic and security issues in the South Asian region. Besides heading BCTR, he is responsible for the Risk Assessment Unit and coordinates number of track 1.5 and track 2 dialogues organised by BIPSS. Mr. Munir completed his undergraduate and graduate studies in International Relations and Strategic Studies at the Australian National University and the S. Rajaratnam School of International Studies at the Nanyang Technological University in Singapore respectively. He has also undertaken executive education programmes at the Harvard Kennedy School on Counter Terrorism and Leadership Development. Mr. Munir is an alumnus of the National Defense University in Washington as well as the Institut Des Hautes Etudes De Défense Nationale (IHEDN) in Paris and Centro Superior de Estudios de la Defensa Nacional (CESEDEN) in Madrid, where he attended Higher Defence Course for Asia Pacific Senior Officers in 2016. In 2019, he was inducted into the Network of Young Asian Security Experts by the Konrad Adenauer Stiftung. He has completed a number of fellowships and was an Indo Pacific Security Studies Fellow at the Daniel K Inouye Asia Pacific Center for Security Studies in Hawaii. He was previously awarded the Distinguished Humphrey Leadership Award Fellowship at Dartmouth College in the U.S. He is a Munich Young Leader of the Munich Security Conference and also the Associate Editor of Peace and Security Review, a quarterly academic journal published by BIPSS.

Dr Naing Swe Oo

Dr Naing Swe Oo is the Founder and Executive Director of the Thayninga Institute for Strategic Studies, a defence think tank established in 2015. He is a graduate of Defence Services Medical Academy, Myanmar. He secured Diploma in Political Studies from Yangon University, Fellowship in Hepatology (Moscow) from Moscow State University. He holds an MBA from Aldersgate College, Philippines. He is also a Ph.D. in Political Science. He previously taught at the Defence Services Medical Academy, Myanmar as an assistant lecturer and also served as a Medical Officer in the Myanmar Army Medical Corps. He is also the publisher and the Editor –in– Chief of Thayninga Weapons and Warfare Magazine, the only magazine focusing on 'Defence Strategies and Military Technologies' in Myanmar. He is also a resource person on defence and security affairs in the Myanmar Institute of Strategic and International Studies (MISIS). His research focus has been on regional security including maritime security, counter terrorism and the peace process of Myanmar.

Shri Asoke K Mukerji, IFS (Retd)

Shri Asoke K Mukerji, IFS (Retd) had served in the United States, the United Kingdom, the Russian Federation, Kazakhstan, United Arab Emirates, Geneva, Soviet Central Asia and the former Yugoslavia before retiring from New York as India's Ambassador and Permanent Representative to the United Nations in December 2015. He was Special Secretary in the Ministry of External Affairs, responsible for International Organizations as well as India's Foreign Policy Planning and Review. In 2017-18, he chaired a multi-stakeholder study group under India's National Security Council Secretariat to recommend cyber norms for India. Shri Mukerji was awarded a Doctor of Civil Laws (*honoris causa*) degree by the University of East Anglia in the UK for his contributions to diplomacy in July 2018. He is a member of the International Institute of Strategic Studies, London. His latest book *"India and the United Nations: a Photo Journey 1945-2015"* was presented by Prime Minister Narendra Modi to the then UN Secretary General Ban Ki-moon in September 2015.

Mrs Dilorom Mamatkulova

Mrs. Dilorom Mamatkulova is a leading Research Fellow at the Institute for Strategic and Regional Studies under the President of the Republic of Uzbekistan. She holds a Master's Degree in International Relations (Global Security), and a Bachelor degree in International Relations, from the University of World Economy and Diplomacy, Tashkent, Uzbekistan. She focuses on problems of international relations and regional security and has extensive experience in cooperation with Asian countries. She is fluent in English, Russian and Uzbek.

Mr Farrukh S Juraev

Mr Farrukh S Juraev is a leading Research Fellow, Head of Department at the Institute for Strategic and Regional Studies under the President of Republic of Uzbekistan, Center for Regional Studies. He was earlier associated with Foundation for Regional Policy (Uzbekistan) and has worked in the Ministry of Justice. He holds Master's Degree in International Relations from the High School of Strategic Analysis and Forecasting, Tashkent, Uzbekistan. He also holds Bachelor of Law from Tashkent State University of Law under the Ministry of Justice, Tashkent, Uzbekistan. He is fluent in English, Russian and Uzbek.

Dr Ajai Sahni

Dr. Ajai Sahni is the Executive Director of the Institute for Conflict Management; the South Asia Terrorism Portal and is also Project Director, IMPACT. He served as a member of the (Madhukar Gupta) Committee on the Restructuring of the Ministry of Home Affairs and is presently a Member of the Police Modernisation and Strengthening Committee, Uttar Pradesh. He has researched and written extensively on issues relating to conflict, politics and development in South Asia, and has participated in advisory projects undertaken for various national and state governments. He jointly edited (with KPS Gill) Terror & Containment: Perspectives on India's Internal Security; The Global Threat of Terror: Ideological, Material and Political Linkages; and separately, The Fragility of Order: Essays in Honour of KPS Gill. He has lectured at numerous professional institutions and appears frequently as an expert on terrorism and insurgency in the Indian and foreign electronic and prints media.

Brig Gen Zakariyya Mansoor

Brigadier General Mansoor is the Director General, Counter Terrorism at the National Counter Terrorism Centre, Ministry of Defence and National Security, Republic of Maldives since 2016. He joined the ranks of Maldives National Defence Force (MNDF) in 1984 and was commissioned eight years later. The General has held various Command and Staff appointments. He has served as the Commandant of MNDF Coast Guard. His earlier command appointments include the Director General of MNDF

Coast Guard, Commanding Officer of Quarter Master Services, Regional Headquarters – S.Gan, Regional Headquarters- Hulhule and Regional Headquarters Lh. Madivaru. General Mansoor has been a key figure in leading Maldives Coast Guard through the rapid transformation and restructuring. In 2014, General Mansoor graduated from the United States National Defence University with a Master of Arts in Strategic and Security Studies. He is also a graduate of the United States Naval Staff College and has also completed Midshipman Course at Royal Naval College, (UK). He has also completed U.S. Coast Guard International Maritime Officers Course, (USA), International Riverine and Coastal Operations Course, (USA), Coast Guard Training Course, (UK), Oil Spill Clearance Course, (UK), Basic Staff Course, (Pakistan), International Search and Rescue Course, Australia, and Maritime Search and Rescue Mission Coordinator Course, (China). He is also a Fellow of the Asia Pacific Centre for Security Studies, (Honolulu, Hawaii).

Lt Gen (Dr) SP Kochhar, AVSM & Bar, SM, VSM (Retd)

Lt Gen (Dr) SP Kochhar, AVSM & Bar, SM, VSM (Retd) served as an independent Director on various governmental and organisational boards, advising on future-proofing of strategic initiatives and intrinsic risk mitigation. He is credited with instituting the 'Telecom Sector Skill' council as a public-private partnership. He effectively collaborated with telecom majors like Airtel, Vodafone etc, and forwarding Indian Government's future agendas of 'Skill India and Digital Literacy'. He is credited for creating a skill ecosystem, comprising of a network of entrepreneurs, and imparting 250 training programmes across the spectrum. He is also on the university boards of Jamia Milia Islamia, Amity and BITS, furthering higher education amongst the youth. He has a Doctorate in trans-disciplinary studies along with a post graduate studies in Engineering from IIT Delhi and Military College. He serves on various committees like Confederation of Indian Industry (CII), Federation of Indian Chambers of Commerce & Industry (FICCI), All India Management Association (AIMA), Ministry of Electronics and Information Technology (MEITY) etc, deliberating on policy formulation and effective implementation.

Mr Andrew Nien-Dzu Yang

Mr. Andrew Nien-Dzu Yang is the Secretary General of the Chinese Council of Advanced Policy Studies (CAPS). He has served as Senior Advisor of the

National Security Council, and Minister for Ministry of National Defense and Vice Minister for Policy, Special Appointment Rank. He has been both the Executive Secretary and a Research Associate with the Sun Yat-sen Center for Policy Studies at National Sun Yat-sen University in Kaohsiung. He was also the Head of International Collaboration and Exchange at National Sun Yat-sen University. From 2000 to September 2009, he was both a Lecturer and Assistant Professor at the General Studies of National Sun Yat-sen University. He is a member of the Heritage Foundation's Asian Studies Center's Advisory Council; also serving as a member of the Executive Committee of the Atlantic Council's Asia-Pacific Strategy Task Force; a member of the International Advisory Council of the Project 2049; and the Taiwan representative of the International SLOC group. He has received his M.Sc. in Economics from the London School of Economics and Political Science in 1981, and for four years he was a Research Associate in Political Economy at Wolfson College, Oxford University (1981-85).

Col Vu Cao Dinh

Col Vu Cao Dinh is the Deputy Director of the Military Science Information Department, Institute for Defence Strategy (IDS), Ministry of National Defence of Vietnam. His primary research interest is in military and security issues of Southeast Asia, including the South China Sea issue. He got his Bachelor of Arts in English from the Military Science Academy in Ha Noi (Vietnam, in 1999) and graduated from the Vietnam Army Academy (in 2013). He also received his Master of Arts in Applied Linguistics from the University of Melbourne, Australia. He attended the Joint Services Command and Staff College, Defence Academy of the United Kingdom in 2014. He has also finished the Advanced Security Cooperation (ASC) course at the Daniel K. Inouye Asia-Pacific Center for Security Studies (DKI APCSS). He is the author of over twenty articles in academic journals.

Dr Roshan Khanijo

Dr Roshan Khanijo is the Assistant Director (Research) at the Centre for Strategic Studies and Simulation (CS3), USI, New Delhi. She is a strategic analyst. Her areas of focus are security, nuclear issues, disarmament and arms control, niche technologies, etc. She has authored, edited books, monographs and occasional papers. She has been a panellist in number of national and international seminars and presented papers in SIPRI, CIISS

(China Institute for International Strategic Studies), Beijing, CICIR (China Institute of Contemporary International Relations) Beijing, Research Institute for National Security Affairs (RINSA), South Korea etc. She has also given guest lecturers at Southern Naval Command, Kochi, Army Training Command (ARTRAC), Shimla, Air War College, Hyderabad, etc.

Mr Amul S. Bahl

Mr. Bahl is an inventor working in various fields. His research extends from the health and wellness sector to air pollution and pathogens that have the potential of Bio Terror. He completed his M.Tech., from Indian Institute of Technology (IIT), Delhi and as an Electrical Engineer, his efforts and R&D was recognized by the President of India. As an educator, he has helped develop 'Andragogy', a system-based learning solution under the 'Skill Educate-Train India' program. He has successfully helped train over 750,000 individuals and enabled them in achieving gainful employment. He is also the author of various books like *Are you wise, Resonate, Candescence*, etc.

Mr Hekmatullah Azamy

Mr Hekmatullah Azamy serves as Deputy Director of the Centre for Conflict and Peace Studies (CAPS). His research is on socio-political and security issues in Afghanistan-Pakistan Region. Further, he has been exclusively focusing on South and Central Asia and how Islamic State (IS) could be a threat to the broader region and Afghanistan. He has written extensively on local and transnational groups operating in and from Afghanistan. He has published articles discussing crime-terror nexus, Taliban relationships with key state and non-state supporters, and the group's ties with other militant groups in the region. Mr Azamy keeps abreast with the development of peace process with the Taliban. He is also a member of several other think tanks including the Central Asia Institute for Strategic Studies (CAISS), based in Kazakhstan.

Ms Aadya Shukla

Ms Aadya Shukla is a Research Scientist & Associate, at MIT Computer Science and Artificial Intelligence Laboratory (CSAIL). Before joining MIT, Aadya served as the Science Technology & Public Policy (STPP) Fellow, at the Belfer Centre, and Harvard Kennedy School (2010-14). Her educational background is in Mathematics, Statistics, Economics, Computer Science & AI, combined with nineteen years of experience of working with both symbolic and non-symbolic AI technologies. She was elected as the prestigious Microsoft Research D.Phil. Scholar at Department of Computer Science, University of Oxford. Aadya won the Cyber-stability Commission Grant, in 2018, to advise the European Union (EU) on "Role of AI and Emerging Technology in Stability of Cyberspace". Her current focus is on cognitive computing, critical infrastructure cybersecurity, trustworthy system design and AI for threat mitigation & national security. Her multiple work-stints (2000-2006) include a Software Engineer (Siemens Ltd. Germany); AI Research Scientist (Cambridge University) and Bioinformatics Scientist (Medical Research Council Oxford).

Maj Gen Ibrahim Manu Yusuf

Maj Gen Ibrahim Manu Yusuf is the Executive Director of the Nigerian Army Resource Centre (NARC) Consult and is in his 34th year of service in the Nigerian Army. He served as a Director at the Kofi Annan International Peacekeeping Training Centre, Accra Ghana, and later as Director, Campaign Planning, at Army Headquarters. He has held appointments at all levels of Command and his appointment prior to joining Resource Centre - was GOC 7 Division of the Nigerian Army, which is the main effort of the Army in the Counter Insurgency Operations in North East Nigeria. There he earned the Nigerian Army Outstanding Operational Command Medal. He is a graduate of the Joint Services Command and Staff College, United Kingdom and National Defence College, Bangladesh. He holds a B.A., degree in History and M.A., Defence Studies from Kings College, London. He has attended numerous professional and academic courses at the Naval Postgraduate School Monterrey, USA, Norwegian Defence International Centre, Norway, and Harvard Kennedy School, Boston, USA amongst others. He has five publications, three contributions to book chapters and two journal publications.

Introduction

Transnational terrorism has emerged as the most formidable threat in the asymmetric wars of the 21ˢᵗ Century. In a generic sense, transnational terrorism implies use of violence for political purposes intended to influence the behaviour of a target group wider than its immediate victims, these groups may act independently or may be controlled or supported by sovereign states in different regions. Transnational terrorism operates simultaneously across continents threatening Westphalian states and modern democratic norms of governance. Transnational terror organisations exploit the flow of people, ideology, weapons and information to further their cause. American academic and former government official Peter Mandeville has written that, Al-Qaeda is one of the first groups to be designated as a transnational terror organisation. Al-Qaeda was successful in expanding its influence among the Pan Islamic Diaspora because they employed ideology to win loyalty and effectively used technology to indoctrinate, recruits cadres, conduct training, plan and coordinate lethal terror strikes across the globe. More often transnational terror groups operate within the vastness of the Grey Zone conflicts, that encompass several hues and shades of terrorism in the political, economic, societal, technological and criminal strains making terrorism a hydra monster.

Transnational terrorism impacts authority of the state, it triggers public disorder, damages trade or foreign direct investment (FDI), stops people to people contact, and cross cultural interaction. Development suffers as funds are diverted for counter terrorism instead of being used for development of industries, infrastructure, education and the health sector. The displacement of population under such circumstances is a natural fallout of prolonged conflict. As per UNHCR in 2007, there were 42.7 million forcibly displaced people, and by the end of 2017 the figure was 68.5 million (UNHCR, 2018). Given the character and ever-changing nature of transnational terrorism, it is imperative to combat it collectively using both kinetic and non-kinetic means. As terrorism becomes transnational it is pertinent to carry out a transnational region wise scan of terrorism to devise an appropriate strategic response to it.

Profiling Transnational Terrorism

The Yemeni-American terrorist Anwar al-Awlaki also called the "Bin Laden of the Internet", in one of his lectures had said that war for the establishment of the Islamic Caliphate is "the Battle of Hearts and Minds". He went on to extort the Jihadis to stay in their own countries and added, "Do not ask for anyone's advice and do not seek anyone's verdict. Kill the disbeliever whether he is a civilian or military, whether that country is in collusion with the West or not, for they have the same ruling. Both of them are disbelievers." The paradigm shift in strategy and character of the conflict from physical to cognitive domain is indicative of political aspirations of a global Jihad for a Caliphate. The Islamic State (IS) has demolished the perception of geographical barriers and has truly acquired the status of transnational terror groups after Al Qaeda. After its ouster from Iraq and Syria and the demise of its physical caliphate, IS remains a battle-hardened and well-disciplined force spread all over in the classic cell structure. It retains leaders, fighters, facilitators, resources and the profane ideology that fuels their efforts". The Islamic State today has extended its network in West Asia, North Africa, Europe, South and East Asia. The IS Affiliates in Greater Sahara and Sahel Corridor are making an effort to establish Islamic State in the Greater Sahara (ISGS). Similarly, the Al Qaeda affiliates are also fighting to maintain foothold in North Africa as part of Al Qaeda in the Islamic Maghreb (AQIM). The complexity in Sahel Corridor is added by web of transnational criminal networks and terror groups that thrive in an environment of weak states, porous borders and humanitarian crisis arising out of displacement of population. Transnational terrorism is spearheaded by foot soldiers with innovative use of cyber, social media, improvised explosive devices, drones and underwater devices. Transnational terrorists are now exploring use of maritime routes to gain access to critical tracts. The targets often have been urban centres and critical infrastructure with a view to attract global attention. The Al Qaeda and IS have been extorting their cadres and sympathisers that it is their religious duty to pursue acquisition of nuclear, biological and chemical weapons to destroy the regimes of disbelievers.

Europe's liberalism and open door policy is facing an acute strain due to refugee influx that is embedded with terrorists. Ironically, the refugees and migrants have not been able to adapt to the new cultural environment of Europe and that is causing communal stress. As per the European Commission more than 5000 EU citizens had joined the Jihadist organisations in Syria and Iraq. The returning cadres are posing serious threat to the European Nations. These radicalised cadres have the potential to act as ideologues and motivators. The threat to Europe is more from the homegrown violent extremism inspired by transnational terror organisations asserting their Islamic identity and way of life within democratic and secular state structure in Europe. Lone wolf, suicidal attacks using licensed weapons and vehicles at public places has become their modus operandi.

The Jihadi terror groups in South East Asia are forging alliances. The Abu Sayyaf Group (ASG) in the Philippines and Jemaah Islamiyah (JI) have shown allegiance to IS and Al Qaeda. The ISIS cadres who returned from Afghanistan, Iraq, and Syria are providing impetus to the faction riddled terror organisations in South East Asia. In Myanmar, Harakah-al-Yaqin (HaY or Faith Movement) and Arakan Rohingya Salvation Army (ARSA) have received support from AQ. Therefore, there is a need to deal with the transnational terrorism in the Middle East and North Africa (MENA), Europe, South Asia and South East Asia in an integrated and coordinated manner.

Af Pak Region remains the epicentre of transnational terrorism. Pakistan is the mother of cross border terrorism against India, Afghanistan and Iran. Pakistan has witnessed a series of sensational terrorist attacks within the country, yet it retains its duplicity in categorising jihadists as good terrorists and bad terrorists. Afghanistan is riddled with a multitude of terrorist groups, Taliban (It has many factions), Islamic State of Khorasan Province (ISKP), Al Qaeda and host of other terrorist organisations. AQIS and ISIS have spread their tentacles in Sri Lanka, Bangladesh and India.

Northern Afghanistan has emerged as a new jihadi frontier. It is well documented that maximum numbers of foreign ISIS cadres hailed from central Asia and Russia. Islamic Movement of Uzbekistan (IMU), Islamic Jihad Union (IJU) and Caucasian Jihadi groups have owed their allegiance to ISKP. Turkmenistan Islamic Party, formerly known as East Turkmenistan Islamic Movement is posing a serious security concern for China in the Xinjiang Province. The Jihadi terrorist groups in Eurasia have the potential to target critical energy and trade and transit infrastructure being developed in the region.

CBRN Threat

The risk of terrorists acquiring fissile material, biological and chemical weapons remain high. The proliferation by Dr AQ Khan of Pakistan cannot be glossed over. There are nuclear weapon states with poor controls over their assets that are infiltrated with Jihadi sympathisers. Poor inventory controls and orphaned fissile materials, chemical agents and biological strains in some of the CIS countries can be used by the terrorist outfits to unleash terror attacks. There is a need to evolve more stringent safeguards and strategies to deal with nuclear terrorism.

Terror Funding

The transnational terror organisations survive on a robust terror funding sources. The major source is through charity, non-governmental organisations working as fronts, shell companies floated by terror groups, illegal activities including extortion, drug trafficking and arms trafficking, human trafficking and sale of natural resources. Eben Kaplan wrote in Council on Foreign Relations about the tentative cost of executing various terror strikes. She wrote, estimated cost of executing 9/11 attack was approximately half a million dollars. 2002 bombing of a Bali nightclub cost about $50,000. The 2004 Madrid train bombing is believed to have cost between $10,000 and $15,000. The 2005 attacks on London's mass transit system cost about $2,000. The funds transfer is also an issue and popular channels for funds transaction are in crypto-currency, hawala and even couriers. The main problem in combatting terror funding is coordinating and reaching common understanding among the global community.

Role of Technology

Technology has made it possible for the terrorists to surmount, geographical and demographic barriers by connecting with likeminded affiliates and cadres through the internet and social media. The Al-Qaida is the best-known transnational terrorist organisation that has used social media and the internet to connect and mobilise likeminded organisations and cadres against perceived common adversaries (Taliban has a vibrant website "Islamic Emirate of Afghanistan"). The evolving technology is being exploited by terror groups to further their perceived cause. Individuals and small groups have the potential to use an array of new and emerging technologies, including drones, self-driven vehicles, autonomous weapon systems, virtual currencies, encrypted communications and Artificial Intelligence (AI) to enhance their reach and lethality. The terrorists are using digital technology at every stage, from recruitment to aligning resources to launching the attacks. The only potent tool for dealing with the terrorism in digital age is smart technology that is emerging as the most important tool for preventing, pre-empting, and responding to terror attacks.

Collaboration in Combatting Transnational Terrorism

The international community will have to fight transnational terrorism bilaterally, multilaterally and through regional and international organisations. Organisations like Shanghai Cooperation Organisation (SCO), BRICS, Turkic Council, The ASEAN Defence Ministers' Meeting (ADMM) and Collective Security Treaty Organization (CSTO) can play a vital role in combatting terrorism. The SCO member states at Bishkek also urged the global community to work towards a consensus on adopting the Comprehensive Convention on International Terrorism (CCIT). Likewise, Financial Action task Force (FATF) can be used more effectively to deal with terror funding. The Nuclear Non-proliferation Treaty (NPT) and the Chemical and Biological Weapons (CBW) non-proliferation treaties should focus on dealing with nuclear, chemical and biological weapons proliferation and take measures to prevent the use of CBW for terrorism. There is a need to put in place mechanism to ensure that all member states should take collective steps to prevent cyber terrorism, share information, maintain data of terror activities and cadres, denial of terror funding through public or private organisations, denial of territories being used for training planning and allowing safe havens.

Under the United Nations the counter terrorism regime lacks a dedicated task force or international endeavour for prevention and mitigation of transnational terror organisations. The overall efforts of the global community for counter terrorism activity lack coherent strategy and policy. Within the United Nations (UN) itself there are more than thirty agencies conducting relevant work on the issue of transnational and international terrorism. Under Chapter VII of the United Nations Charter, compliance with Resolution 1267 should be enforced to cease support for terrorists, close training camps and end illegal weapons and narcotics trade. The UN Counter-Terrorism Implementation Task Force (CTITF) consisted of 38 international entities which by virtue of their work have a stake in multilateral counter terrorism efforts. There is a need to implement the recommendations of the UN Counter-Terrorism Implementation Task Force (CTITF) especially in dealing with the movement of foreign terrorists' fighters, terror financing, strengthening of legal system for the involvement of terrorists in another country and sharing of intelligence of terror attacks. All countries that keep relations with the terror organisations and institutions supporting terror outfits must face international sanctions. Therefore, any violation must invite more stringent economic and diplomatic sanctions. The UN thus, should be the overarching organisation to deal with transnational terrorism.

Special Address

Shri Kanwal Sibal, IFS (Retd)

Transnational terrorism has acquired global attention and it has now become a major disruptive factor. Terrorism of any kind be it cross border or transnational, is a serious challenge to the modern states. State sponsored terrorism may not have international implications, but transnational terrorism does have global implications. Trans-border terrorism targets civilians to create a sense of terror and make headlines. It affects citizenry and also the quality of life. The costs to the society have been huge, especially, for democratic states, and it impacted security and freedom of citizens. Cross border terrorism in Kashmir has put restrictions on people, curbing their freedom of movement and activities that citizens are supposed to enjoy.

Transnational terrorism is backed in most cases by religious ideology. Pakistan has used cross border terrorism to create instability in J&K. Transnational terrorists are non-state actors. In reality, however, there are no non-state actors, as these often operate and get support from a state and the state then becomes their safe havens. There are a few cases where transnational terror organisations create a territorial space for themselves, majorly due to state sponsorship. In case of Pakistan, it has used terrorism as state policy, but in the recent past, it too has faced challenges from the same terror organisations. Pakistan has used military power to gain control of the Western parts, which was slowly slipping out of the government control. Similarly, Pakistan is also in control of Pakistan Occupied Kashmir (POK) where it is nurturing Lashkar-e-Taiba (LeT), Jaish-e-Muhammad (JeM) and other radical organisations to perpetrate terror attacks on India. We have seen deadly attacks by LeT and JeM such as the 26/11 Mumbai attack and the Pathankot Air base attack. The rise of 'Islamic State' is the result of some states who have given space to non-state actors to become terrorists and to establish a Caliphate. The creation of Islamic State was due to lack of commitment by the global community to address this challenge, the outcome of lack of seriousness of the global community. There are regional, geopolitical and geostrategic reasons for the rise of Islamic State. After the Islamic State posed threat to the modern Westphalia States, there has been a change in the global thinking; as a result, some actions were taken on ground by the U.S., Russia and other countries. President Putin was aware of the threat from Islamic terrorists and he had stated that he will prefer to fight Islamic Jihadists in Syria, rather than on its own soil. Russia saw the cost of fighting Islamic State in Syria lower than fighting it on its own soil. The equation of Saudi Arabia and UAE has also changed, and now they too see it as a threat to them.

Boko Haram has come into existence due to the Tribal issues which has developed into a serious threat in Nigeria, along with the spread of Al Qaeda ideology in this part of the world. Unfortunately, the North African Nations have been left alone to fight this menace. The root of this problem is spread of Wahhabi Islam and Muslim Brotherhood. The Islamic State may have been destroyed but the ideology has not been destroyed. The fight now has become more challenging since we are battling an amorphous and faceless organisation.

Transnational terrorism has to have transnational ideology for wider traction, but local terrorism has local causes and reasons. Unfortunately, transnational terrorism has resonated from the Muslim world. Transnational terrorism has another major problem especially, if the terrorists take refuge in other countries, then elimination becomes extremely difficult. However, the U.S. did assassinate Osama Bin Laden, by violating the sovereign territory of another nation. Cross border terrorism has become a state policy of Pakistan and a challenge for India. During the Soviet occupation of Afghanistan, the jihadis had come from across the globe, but when Soviets returned, the kind of turmoil those jihadis had created in their homeland, was another major consequence of using Jihadists for geo-strategic reasons.

Radicalisation is another major problem, because it is very difficult to identify when people get radicalised. It is extremely difficult and challenging for the state to control the knowledge being shared in Madrasas, as also monitor social media activities and their influence. Thus, radicalisation is a serious challenge to the states. It is for the Islamic society to ensure that youths do not get radicalised. The Islamic society needs to introspect as Islam cannot be portrayed as a base for spread of violence.

Social media has become a major source of self-radicalisation. Criminals and terror organisations are always ahead of the government in exploiting technology and social media for their divisive purposes. As the influence of media and social media spreads to even the remotest areas, there is now no need for close physical proximity for radicalisation.

North Korea has been considered a rogue state due to its Nuclear Weapon programme. Baloch National Army is also considered a terrorist organisation. But, Pakistan, despite repeatedly using Taliban and other terrorists as state policy against India and Afghanistan has not been recognised as a threat. Unfortunately, Pakistan receives Chinese supports, especially on matters of terror. This is the underlining reason for not declaring Azhar Mahmood a terrorist.

The Financial Action Task Force (FATF) has failed to nail Pakistan despite Pakistan's deep involvement in supporting the terror organisations. China has been selective in her approach to deal with terrorism. Now with China taking over the Chair of the FATF, it will be even more difficult to declare Pakistan in the blacklist of states supporting terror organisations. Turkey has been using non-state actors for leveraging its position as leader of the Islamic Nations. Saudi Arabia has modified her outlook with regard to her support to the radicals and Islamic terror organisations. Selective response against terrorism by global community is detrimental to the global peace and stability. Terror organisations have been quick to use technology to undertake terror attacks. Denial of technology to terror organisations may not be possible but use of technology to counter and prevent acts of terror must be the endeavour.

PART - I

Transnational Terrorism in Asia and Beyond

1

ISIS Mutation as Transnational Terrorist Threat

Dr Waiel S.H. Awwad

Introduction

The desire for oil and gas has shifted the sphere of dominance initially from Europe to America-Israel, and now to Russia and China. The unrest has got exacerbated with the discovery of more oil and gas in the Mediterranean, shared by Syria, Egypt, Lebanon, Palestine, Cyprus and Israel. Further, Turkey and Iran saw the turbulence in the Middle East, as an opportunity, to increase their sphere of influence in the region.

The revival of Islamist movement in the Middle East is seen as an instrument, to achieve political goals and discourage democracy, liberalism and above all, counter all these political movements in the Middle East. The war on terrorism, in fact, has been used as a pretext to invade the countries, launch wars and create sectarian conflicts, especially, in the Middle East and South Asia. Mrs Hilary Clinton in her testimony had stated that the "Good Al-Qaeda" was created to defeat the Soviet Union by the U.S.–ISI-AL Saud conglomeration. When the then USSR withdrew from Afghanistan and the U.S. decided to make military bases in Saudi Arabia, U.S. sponsored Mujahedeen turned the guns against their masters. However, post the terrorist attacks of September 11th, they were labelled as the 'Bad Al-Qaeda' and were branded as terrorist organisation.

Al-Qaeda had established its presence in Iraq and Syria during the American occupation of Iraq. The turbulence on the ground was exploited by Al Qaeda and ISIS to establish areas of influence in both these countries. The defeat of terrorist organisations in Iraq and Syria, (namely Al-Qaeda and ISIS), may be a sign of relief for the people of the region, but it did not make the world safer. Still a large number of terrorist related acts have been visible around the world, from France, Saudi Arabia to Iran, Britain, Nigeria, Somalia, Yemen, Sri Lanka, Philippines and Afghanistan.

Pledging Loyalty to Al–Baghdadi

Afghanistan and Iraq invasion revived Arab Nationalism and ideology of Muslim Brotherhood, which are aligned with Jihadist ideology. They received proxy support from the regional and extra-regional players to trigger jihad in their respective countries. They have established new networks in Yemen, Maghreb and some have joined the U.S. forces in Afghanistan, as well as Iraq. Abu Musab Al Zarqawi, a follower of Bin Laden and Ayman Al Zawahiri, was made in charge, to wage Jihad in Syria and Iraq. He had recruited Iraqi victims of sectarian violence into his network. The main objective was to gain loyalty and to spread both awe and fear among the people, so that they could then dominate and take the lead to establish Islamic State. However, Bin Laden was against premature declaration of Islamic State in Iraq.

The so-called 'Islamic State' declared by Abu Baker Al Baghdadi, opened the door for the Al-Qaeda's franchise groups, to start recruitments, and many joined the organisation. Though ideology was same, but the implementation differed. ISIS was ruthless and more radical, as they adopted the Salafist-Wahhabi religious practice and denounced democracy and secularism. Therefore, Islamic State turned against other sects of Sunni Islam as well.

The ISIS cadres were relocated to Syria and Iraq via Turkey, with full knowledge of President Erdogan, who had opened the Turkish border with Syria for training and arming the new Jihadist group. After the defeat of Daesh (ISIS), the President of Turkey, had transported the survivors to Libya, promised 2000 USD/month, including Turkish citizenship after six months of indulgence in fighting. This also proved that the Jihadist groups under the umbrella of President Erdogan were able to mobilise and transport them to an unstable country, to achieve political objectives.

Turkey has played a major role in spreading political Islam and was viewed as a model to be implemented in different Arab States. This was supposedly done with a belief that Muslim Brotherhood will bring back the 'Islamic Glory', a modern Caliph, which can unite the Arab and Muslim countries, as it was under the Ottoman Empire in the past. The idea of creating modern Ottoman Empire gave fillip to the Jihadists ideology, to reclaim erstwhile Ottoman territory in Europe and Middle East as well. So, many mercenaries had started their journey back to Europe through Turkey, using the same route they entered into Syria. As a result, there was a sudden revival of radicalisation among Muslim citizens in Europe and even in Middle East and North Africa (MENA).

Reasons for Joining the Terror group

Money - Mohd Rashid Ridha had stated that "There is money in the affairs". Hasan Al Banna (1905-1945) was his student who established the Muslim Brotherhood movement in Egypt. The promise of a stable income in an otherwise war-ravaged country, lured the youth to join ISIS and Al Qaeda. The families of these young recruits were also guaranteed a hefty compensation in case they were killed. The ISIS and Al Qaeda leadership took advantage of unemployment, lack of skills leading to lack of hope amongst the youth to lead a successful life. The radical Imams had found a fertile ground in these countries to recruit mercenaries and send them to fight in Libya, Syria, Iraq and other countries. It had become a good industry for Imams and source of good earning for unskilled youths and criminals.

Loyalty - The franchise groups of Al-Qaeda had pledged loyalty to Al Baghdadi and in many cases switched sides.

State Sponsorship - No real battles were fought against the Islamic State. The flattened cities foretold a different story of the actual reasons behind the carnage. Further, they also questioned the fact that where all these mercenaries had disappeared. It may not be revealed where all these Jihadists disappeared, and further, by the time they resurfaced, it had become just an academic exercise. However, supposedly, according to intelligence reports, thousands of them were relocated to Libya, Yemen, and Afghanistan and some could have been located to Commonwealth of Independent States (CIS). These proxies will emerge when next target country is known; it could be Iran, where these forces may converge from Afghanistan, CIS or even Saudi Arabia.

Ideology - The support to radical movements started as early as the 18th century, the ideology of Wahhabism in the Arab Peninsula was followed by Al Saud tribe, who had conquered the Peninsula. Ambassador Dore Gold had explained the link between the current global terrorism and jihadists strategy in his book titled *"Hatred's Kingdom: How Saudi Arabia supports the New Global Terrorism"*. Gold had spoken about Wahhabism, which is the foundation of Saudi State: "the struggle between Saudi pan-Islamism and Nasserism (Jamal Abdul Naser) had other side effects that had lasted for decades". It was Saudi Arabia who revived Islamic fundamentalism in Egypt and in the rest of the Arab countries. It was used as a tool to topple secular leaders and thwart any Arab leader movement to unite the Arabs.

The Salafist-Wahhabi Agenda

The Wahhabi–Salafist ideology is based on four key issues, that they propagate to pursue their objective and to establish the Islamic State. First, kill all non-believers or apostates, second, all must accept Islam or become Muslim, third, modern Democratic States or Sultanates are unlawful and fourth, single Caliph across the globe.

Multinational companies have transnational interests and it had appeared that liberals had won the race, and their Doctrine dominated the world scene, especially, the 'Neorealist School of Thought'. But Saudi Arabia's attempt to spread Wahhabi Islam was seen by the U.S. as an opportunity to use the radicals to pursue their own strategic objectives of controlling energy security, by deploying these assets in target countries. Mr. Christopher Davidson had in his book *"Shadow Wars: The Secret Struggle for the Middle East"* stated that "CIA regards ISIS-Al Qaeda as a strategic but volatile asset to be wielded against their enemy". Saudi Arabia has exploited their relations with the U.S. to create their own power centre within the Islamic world. Mr Rachel Bronson, in his *"Thicker than Oil"*, has spoken of U.S. allowing Saudi Monarch to do so, and signing an accord, to protect Al Saud tribe. The U.S. still considers Saudi as an asset to keep Russians out of the Middle East and had admitted to spending $500 million to train 500 "moderate rebels" in Syria and all but five of them had defected to Al Qaeda in Syria. This was a wake up call for all those who believed that a regime change will work by employing terrorism as a tool.

The Main Reasons for the Spread of Violent Extremism and Terrorism

(a) Military action in Libya, Yemen, Somalia, Syria and Iraq.

(b) Lack of democracy, corrupt governments, grievances, injustice, poverty, illiteracy and economic austerity measures.

(c) Glory – where people were looking for a slot in the centre stage and to take revenge.

(d) Fake paradise and lack of religious knowledge.

(e) Social media as a tool for radicalisation and Online recruitment.

(f) Building network and use of media to execute operations.

(g) Extreme ideology - According to reports 90 percent of the curriculum in schools run by ISIS in Raqqa, Syria, Mosul, Iraq were based on Wahhabi Ideology as also in textbooks of Saudi schools.

The killing of Al Baghdadi could start the beginning of a new era. IS will mutate the terrorist organisation in different parts of the world and will challenge the established norms and politics. Extremism, terrorism and Jihadist are returning to Afghanistan, since the U.S. is using Islamic militancy as a tool for its foreign policy. Further, Daesh is re-grouping in Iraq after the U.S. forces killed their top leaders namely - Al Mohandes, leader of People Mobilisation Unit (PMU) in Iraq, and Iranian Army Commander Major General Qassem Soleimani, Head of Al-Quds Forces. Both forces have fought the terrorist organisations and have defeated them in Syria and Iraq. The jubilation was evident in areas harbouring remaining cadres of the terror network, as they had started changing their warfare strategy and resorting to guerrilla tactics, thus, taking advantage of the geography. It had also relied on sleeper cells around the world and had decentralised Command to carry out terrorist activities. The aim of ISIS is to project itself as the only organisation to lead the Jihadist culture, protect 'Muslim Umma' and recover, under the auspices of the global terrorist system. What will help the terror group is the sedition policy established in Iraq and Syria and instigated further by the presence of foreign occupation forces, which will not only propagate both the governments' anti-Sunni agenda but also ISIS propaganda such as 'apostate regimes and Sunni-defendant' organisations.

"Who Cooks Poison will Taste it Ultimately"

It is an end of an era and birth of a new one and the new trajectory will be along South and South-East Asia. The global war on terror must be fought on all fronts collectively by exposing the intentional errors of invested parties. It is possible to win this war when countries stop sponsoring terrorism, deny safe havens and support to the violent extremists. The defeat of the ISIS in Syria and Iraq does not indicate the end of terrorism as the ideology is not defeated yet. In fact it is gaining in strength and multiplying in different parts of the world. It is a painful reminder that the fight against terrorism is delusionary. Finally, defeating terrorism is only possible, if states stop using it as a tool of foreign policy.

2

Islamophobia and Reactionary Terrorism in America

Prof Carol M Burke

To understand the threats of terrorism we must not only focus on violence carried out in the name of radical religious belief; but also devote the same rigor to the examination of ways in which the alienated, the fearful, and the disgruntled, (with little faith in their National Government and its institutions), find innocent scapegoats in whom they invest their rage. These are American extremists who cling to the last shreds of a racialised identity in a changing world. Most of them are radical conservatives who consider themselves as part of a coalition called the "alternative right" or the "alt-right." We might describe the acts of intimidation they direct indiscriminately at representatives of minority groups as reactionary terrorism; designed to draw attention to perceived injustice and ultimately to dismantle the present order. This they do by blocking progressive initiatives, intimidate minority communities, and restore an idealised past, bleached of all colour except red, white, and blue.

The U.S. General Accounting Office (GAO) began collecting statistics on lethal terrorist attacks on September 12, 2001, the day after hijacked planes flew into the World Trade Center towers. This governmental watchdog agency has reported that between September 12, 2001, and January 2019, 73% of lethal terrorist attacks on American soil were the work of right-wing extremists.[1] We can track some of this terrorism to the

---

1   Had the report included attacks that produced several injuries but no deaths, the percentage would have been higher. Also missing are the 244 cases of school shooting that took place during the same time period, shootings like the one at Virginia Tech in

rising advocacy of white supremacy and White Nationalism trumpeted by the alt-right.

Whether targeting Muslims, Jews, African-Americans, Latinos, Sikhs, or whether acting singly or as a group, these terrorists transform fear and resentment into retaliatory violence. In assembling the puzzle that is terrorism in America today, we need to develop a keen understanding of what these ultra-right terrorists share, what they believe, how they acquire those beliefs or spread them to others, what they seek to achieve, and the tactics they employ. One must resist the temptation to simplify. Instead, one must employ multi-disciplinary methods to understand the historical, economic, psychological, and the political contexts, to this domestic terrorism. One must look at the grievances that, when knitted together, form a potent sense of victimhood, that can threaten our peace and security.

I would like to stress that seeking to understand this home-grown terrorism is in no way a denial of the threat posed by foreign or domestic jihadists willing to use terrorism to advance their cause.[2] One must be vigilant, for example, in the efforts to thwart an attack directed at the U.S. or at U.S. Personnel abroad by ISIS in retaliation for the killing of Abu-Bakr al-Baghdadi. The problem is larger and more complicated, and that it is an over-simplification, to think of transnational terrorism and domestic terrorism as two completely different phenomena. To understand one, we must understand its relationship with others, even if that relation is a reactionary one. Only then can one interpret the all-too prevalent terrorism erupting in our schools, our places of worship, in our workplaces and public gathering places.

In other words, my remarks will try to show briefly, that unreflective reaction to the threat of violence, can produce its own violence and that racist rhetoric can legitimise the hateful precepts of radical ideology, thereby, inviting on stage what has been relegated to the wings for many

---

which 33 university students were massacred, or the horror in Newtown Conn that took the lives of 20 first grade students, 6 and 7 year-olds, along with 8 adults, and the one at a high school in Texas in which 17 high school students in Texas were murdered.

2   The 9/11 attacks can be seen as the importing of the political as well as religious, but they were certainly not the first such terrorist acts committed on American soil. One only need to look at the murders, attempted murders, kidnappings, and bombings at abortion clinics by religious fundamentalists like the followers of The Army of God, attacks that began in the 1980's.

years. The jihadist and those who hate him have a good deal in common. Although the alt-right in America trades attitudes and tactics with the far right in Europe, my remarks will focus on the U.S., a Nation that is still coming to terms with the aftermath of the hijackings that took place eighteen years ago.

September 11, 2001 had exposed American vulnerability not just to all Americans but to the world. A month later, America was at war in Afghanistan, and seventeen months after that at war in Iraq. Al-Qaeda hijackers had not sneaked into the U.S. from Canada or Mexico; they were living in the U.S. on bona fide visas. Fifteen had come from Saudi Arabia, one from Egypt, two from the U.A.E., and one from Lebanon; none had come from Afghanistan or Iraq, the Nations whose regimes we would topple and whose peace, in the midst of civil wars we would vainly struggle to restore. The horror of the 9/11 terrorists had inflicted upon the U.S. that September morning--the deaths of 2,977 and the injuries to 6000- had caused America to freeze in horror. We all remember watching the loop of the dramatic self-monumentalising video as the first flight and then shortly the next one struck the Twin Towers in New York.

On that day, it was known that one should prepare for other terrorist attacks to come, attacks from hostile enemies from the Middle East, about whom we understood little. What one did not know was that most of the atrocities would be committed by individuals in sympathy with radical beliefs, rather than by those operating at the behest of jihadist organisations. What one did not knew was that most of the attackers would be U.S. citizens. What we did not understand is how quickly and how vehemently hatred, fuelled by incessant televised looping of violence and victims, the contagion of incendiary memes on social media and in public discourse, could incite rage against innocents and enfranchise a whole host of perceived injustices.

American Justice System treats those who commit domestic terrorism differently, from those who commit foreign or foreign-inspired jihadist terrorism. One does not prosecute them under the same laws, and don't even use the same words to describe similar acts. For example, giving support to a domestic and violent white supremacist group like Atomwaffen is not against the law, whereas giving support to the PKK, the Kurdish Workers Party, is against the law, because the PKK is on the State Department's list of terrorist organisations, all of which are foreign. There have been attempts to designate some white supremacist groups with a track record of violence as "terrorist groups," but Conservatives in Congress have objected to the use of the word "terrorist" when applied to white supremacists, so these hate groups continue under the umbrella of the First Amendment. FBI funding earmarked to investigate white supremacists has been reduced in the last few years as has funding for programs designed to help those individuals, who wish to leave hate groups and transition into mainstream culture.

It was natural for Americans to feel shock, fear, and anger in the aftermath of 9/11. What is unnatural is the way in which fear and insecurity have been cultivated by nativist partisans, to justify and provoke extremist counter-violence. One expression of that insecurity is Islamophobia, a term generally used to describe a pervasive fear and hatred of Islam. This can manifest itself in individuals or display group hostility, abuse (physical or verbal), threats of abuse, and violence directed towards Muslims, their property, and the places where they worship. Islamophobia found fallow ground not only in the racism of the far right, but also in the mainstream.

By 2008, Islamophobia had blossomed into several well-organised anti-Muslim groups. One of the most influential was the "Birther Movement" designed to discredit the campaign of Barack Obama, the first person of colour to represent a major party in his run for president. The talk shows' hosts on right-wing radio couldn't get enough of it. Billboards appeared. Despite ample evidence to the contrary, the Birther Movement had claimed that Obama was not Christian as he insisted but was secretly Muslim. Birthers maintained that he was not 'native born,' a requirement for any President, stipulated in the constitution. After all, Obama has an African-sounding surname, and some Birthers were convinced that his middle name, Hussein, was the same as the powerful Muslim leader of Iraq whom U.S. forces overthrew in 2003 and was ample proof that he was Muslim. It didn't matter to them that there is no religious requirement for the President of the United States. Nor did it matter that Obama was born in Hawaii, two years after it became a state. It didn't matter that his white American mother and black African father were students at the University of Hawaii when he was born. It didn't matter that then-candidate Obama had produced a certified birth certificate and a birth announcement from a local paper at the time. It didn't matter that his father's homeland, Kenya, is 83 per cent Christian. It didn't matter that although his father was born to Muslim parents, Barack Obama Sr, had converted to Anglicanism, when he went as a child to an Anglican school and later in his life was an avowed atheist. Ironically, no one had questioned the natural-born status or religious affiliation of Obama's opponent, John McCain. McCain was born in Panama while his father was stationed in the Canal Zone, then under U.S. control but not a state.

The most prominent and the loudest leader of the Birther movement was Donald Trump, and several Republican members of Congress. They were complicit in keeping the doubts about Obama's lineage alive. It is not clear whether the leaders of the movement really believed the bigotry they were spouting or were simply cynical manipulators of their conspiracy-driven followers. You spread the same story enough times, and eventually many will believe that there might be some truth to it.

Donald Trump has added fuel to the racist fire in America. During his campaign for the President, he promised to prohibit all Muslims from immigrating to America. Eleven days after Trump won his campaign for President in 2016, Richard Spencer, founder of the alt-right and the new face of white supremacy in America addressed a meeting of the National Policy Institute, an all-white organisation he created, with a Nazi salute to Trump: "Hail Trump. Hail our people. Hail our victory." Spencer had made clear what Trump's campaign slogan would be, "Make America Great Again," meant to the alt-right: "America was, until this past generation a white country designed for us and our posterity. It belongs to us. It is our creation; it is our inheritance, and it belongs to us. To be white is to be a striver, a crusader, an explorer and a conqueror... For us as Europeans, it is only normal when we are great again.[3]"

What Spencer and other racists always fail to acknowledge is that the creation of an America as white as cotton, went hand-in-hand with the right to own men and women strictly on the basis of their skin colour.

Trump had refused to condemn the neo-Nazis demonstrating in Charlottesville, Virginia on August 11, 2017, at a 'Unite the Right' rally at which one of the white supremacists used his car as a weapon to attack a group of counter protesters, killing one and injuring 19. Trump has re-tweeted racist propaganda several times and has also chosen close advisors,

---

3   Spencer, Richard. "Address to the Annual Meeting of the National Policy Institute, Washington D.C., November 19, 2016. https://www.youtube.com/watch?v=1o6-bi3jlxk

many fellow members of the anti-Muslim / white supremacy groups. Further, and his words have been quoted by the El Paso, TX shooter who in August killed 22 on a rampage against 'Hispanics' and by the Christ Church shooter in New Zealand, who killed 54 worshiping Muslims. Like the white supremacists whom Richard Spencer leads, Trump had seen no reason to honour the American generosity inscribed on the tablet on the Statue of Liberty:

> "Give me your tired, your poor, your huddled masses yearning to breathe free, The wretched refuse of your teeming shore. Send these, the homeless, tempest-tossed to me; I lift my lamp beside the golden door!"

The lamp is clearly gone out and the golden door closed shut, or in Trump's words, "America is full." He has repeatedly described those seeking entrance as "invaders," "rapists," "disease ridden," "violent criminals," "animals," and other "bad hombres" from "shithole countries." When four women of colour in the House of Representatives criticised his views this year; Trump responded, "So interesting to see 'Progressive' Democrat Congresswomen, who originally came from countries whose governments are a complete and total catastrophe, the worst, most corrupt and inept anywhere in the world (if they even have a functioning Government at all), now loudly and viciously telling the people of the United States, the greatest and most powerful Nation on earth, how our government is to be run....Why don't they go back and help fix the totally broken and crime infested places from which they came."

Not only did Trump invoke an ugly and old American racist slur ("Go back where you came from"), but he has somehow failed to realise that three of the four Congress Women were born in America. Racism does not countenance historical facts nor invoke the constitutional principles on which the Nation was founded. Racist Presidential rhetoric dispensed through a Twitter account with 50 million viewers and slurs that cast brown and black Americans as threats to our Nation, only legitimise white nationalist hatred and embolden some to turn their hate into violence.

After 9/11, anti-Muslim hate groups have made no distinctions between Jihadists/Islamists and the Muslims who worship down the street at the local mosque. To them, all Muslims are radicals, whether overtly or clandestinely, seeking to abolish the American legal system and install

Sharia Law, doing so with their own army of infiltrators, the Muslim Brotherhood, individuals whom the alt-right sometimes insists has already infiltrated the FBI, the State Department, and the halls of Congress.

In 2007, Brigitte Gabriel, the head of the most powerful anti-Muslim organisation, ACT for America, and the major lobbyist for state-sponsored anti-Sharia laws, put it this way:

> A practicing Muslim who believes the word of the Koran to be the word of Allah, who abides by Islam, who goes to mosque and prays every Friday, who prays five times a day — this practicing Muslim, who believes in the teachings of the Koran, cannot be a loyal citizen of the United States."[4]

In 2017, Gabriel was invited to the White House to meet the President Trump; a fact that was first denied by White House staff but then admitted to, when Gabriel posted a photo of her there. The charge that she and others on the alt-right have made--that the belief in a specific religion is incompatible with citizenship. This is the very argument that the Ku Klux Klan and other anti-Catholic hate groups made against Catholics arriving on American shores at the turn of the 20th Century.

Neither Brigitte Gabriel nor Donald Trump is a terrorist, yet the far reach of their inflammatory rhetoric can encourage others to take up arms against the threats they fear minority groups harbour. Ironically, anti-Muslim extremists have a good deal in common with their jihadist counterparts. Both groups see their struggle as one for purity— one group for racial purity, and the other for religious purity. Both groups rely on a revisionist history, which allows them to construct an idealised past. For Jihadists, that past was in 7thC Arabia and at the time of the Prophet Muhammad. For many white supremacists, it was when white men had ruled America, when slaves were not free, and when women did not have the right to vote. Other white nationalists hanker to return to post-WWII America when men in their twenties made their way home from the war in Europe and the Pacific to take their jobs back from the women, who had held them in their absence. Many had moved out of the cities and into the suburbs and had started families ready to realise their American dream. This was a time when a new cult of domesticity took hold in America.

---

4   From a June 2007 lecture Gabriel gave to at the U.S. Joint Forces Staff College and broadcast on C-SPAN.

Like jihadists, white supremacists have regarded the roles men and women occupy as distinct. Women are assigned exclusively to the domestic sphere, giving birth to and raising the next generation ready to join the struggle. Both jihadists and white supremacists spurn democracy. They see their quest as sacred and themselves as the most ardent patriots or the staunchest zealots. Both recruit young males in search of a cause to cling to. To the alienated, Western male with few social interactions in the actual world, one who lives a solitary life on-line, they promise direction and incorporation in a greater brotherhood. Their propaganda works to inspire both the lone wolf, whom police often describe as the 'self-radicalised' terrorist, and the recruit interested in joining the fraternity. The latter recruits are those they train militarily. Both groups stockpile military-style weapons: the jihadists for the battle at hand, the alt-right extremists for the race war that is to come. Both groups want their demonstrations of power to awaken a sleeping world. They seek to be the stars of their own performances by announcing their attacks seconds before it is done, by posting manifestos, photos, and videos for cyber consumption worldwide.

Islamophobia is just another branch of the family of white supremacy, groups who view whites as both intellectually and morally superior to those with darker skin. Throughout American history, hate groups have come out of their caves in times of social change, times that seem to deny the respect and prosperity that they feel was their birth right. What we have seen in America in the 21st century is a perfect storm of social change: from the influx of immigrants to a changing demography (by 2045, whites will comprise less than 50 percent of all Americans), from the Great Recession in 2007-09 in which 10 million Americans lost their homes, to the ever-widening inequality gap, from the massive loss of working class jobs to the weakening of labour unions, from more women and minorities assuming jobs historically, held by white men to the growth of social media platforms as back alleys for the expressions of resentment and rage. Even though 9-11 is 18 years behind us, with all these changes, some Americans still feel terribly vulnerable and that the social contract they've been offered is a tattered one. This is not to excuse for their outbursts of reactionary terrorism but merely an attempt to explain it.

3

Mapping the Terror in North Africa

Prof Usman A Tar

The transformation of the world into a 'Global Village' ensures that there are no sharper differences in the operations of local terrorist groups, as their activities now transcend National borders. This increasing inter-connectedness of global societies also paves way for the international movement of people and illegal weapons from one country to another. Accordingly, the link between terrorist organisations characterises one of the essential fundamentals of modern terrorism.[1] In Africa, this scenario is perfectly played out in the Sahel region, which has become the epicentre of Jihadism in Africa, as Islamist groups such as Boko Haram, Islamic State in West Africa (ISWAP) among others, have continued to leverage on the massive and relatively empty area to hide, recruit and coordinate their terrorist agenda.[2]

Consequently, the recognition of these evolving security challenges has opened new spaces for security responses across Africa, resulting in the integration of counter terrorism strategies as key components of national, regional and continental security architecture.[3] In the case of the Lake Chad Basin, the emergence of new regional security architecture to fight terrorism is not totally novel, it is built on an existing regional integration

---

1   Asafa, J. (2010). "Conceptualizing and Theorizing Terrorism in the Historical and Global Context", Humanity and Society. Vol. 34(4). Pp. 317-338.

2   Pujol-Mazzini, A. (2018). "Islamist groups turn their attention to West Africa", The Washington Post, July 3, 2018.

3   Flemes,D. & Lobell,S.E. (2015). 'Contested Leadership in InternationalRelations',Intern ational Politics 52 (42):139- 45.

bloc – the Lake Chad Basin Commission (LCBC) was founded in 1964. However, recent efforts by some members of the LCBC to create a new regional security architecture, under the aegis of the Multinational Joint Task Force (MJTF), to fight terrorism, has led to a paradigm shift in security regionalisation within the Basin.[4]

Therefore, this paper examines evolving transnational terrorists' threats in the Lake Chad Basin and the counter terrorism strategies being adopted by the Member States to counter these threats. The paper is divided into five sections. The first section is the introduction, followed by the conceptual and theoretical framing. In the third section, we map the dynamics of transnational terrorism in the Lake Chad region. The fourth section dwells on the regional security strategies for countering terrorism in the sub region. The final section is the concluding thoughts on the paper.

Conceptual Discourse and Theoretical Framing of Terrorism

The Terrorist Financing Convention (TFC) in Article 2(1) (b) describes terrorism as:

> Any … act intended to cause death or serious bodily injury to a civilian, or to any other person not taking an active part in the hostilities in a situation of armed conflict, when the purpose of such act, by its nature or context, is to intimidate a population, or to compel a Government or an international organisation to do or to abstain from doing any act.[5]

Thus, terrorism involves a combination of distinct forms of violence and motivation. While the violence is such that causes death or serious bodily harm to civilians or non-combatants, the motivations are inclinations to either instil widespread fear or to influence the actions of governments or international organisations.[6] A common denominator in all its manifestations is that, as a strategic choice, terrorism follows a three-stage method: disorientation; target response and gaining

---

4   Tar, U.A. & Bala, B. (2018).Boko Haram Insurgency, Terrorism and the Challenges of Peace building in the Lake Chad Basin. In Omeje, K.C. (Ed.). Peace building in Contemporary Africa: In Search of Alternative Strategies. London: Routledge.

5   United Nations (1999) *International Convention for the Suppression of Terror Financing, 1999.* Retrieved: www.un.org (Accessed on 25th October, 2106), pp.3

6   Davis, K. (2003). "Legislating Against the Financing of Terrorism: Pitfalls & Prospects". *Journal of Financial Crime.* Vol. 10(3). Pp. 269-74.

legitimacy. From several other approaches that exist to terrorism; scholars, international organisations and countries have arrived at varying working albeit imperfect definitions of terrorism. However, for the purpose of this discourse, the approach encapsulated in Article 2(1) (b) of the Terrorist Financing Convention is adopted as a working definition.

Counter Terrorism and Counter-Insurgency (CT-COIN)

This is a concept that juggles the practices, tactics, techniques, and strategies that governments, militaries, police departments and corporations adopt in response to terrorist threats and/or acts, both real and attributed.[7] It also refers to the domestic military and legal measures put in place by the government of any state to prevent and counter terrorism in collaboration with sub-regional, regional and continental organisational instruments. This is achieved by intercepting communications, monitoring internet and social media habits and blocking access to terrorist training materials, funding and building of genetic capacity of the national criminal justice system. Counter terrorism refers to multifaceted measures or operations, which can be adopted internally within a Nation, or across borders in conjunction with other international bodies or agencies, to deal with the threat of terrorism. To effectively implement counter terrorism strategies, it is necessary that the perception of the terrorists and the victims of acts of terror, whether directly or indirectly must be adjudged and ascertained. Terrorism could be committed by armed groups or individuals of an armed group within a nation; with or without external collaborations.[8]

Theoretical Framing

There are several theoretical frameworks that might be applied to understand transnational terrorism and counter terrorism approaches. However, in this paper, we shall dwell on *'Radicalisation Theory'* for an analysis of transnational terrorism and the *'Regional Security Complex Theory (RSCT)'*, as the theoretical model upon which the Lake Chad Basin regional counter terrorism strategy is grounded.

---

7   Alagappa, M. (1995).'Regionalism and Conflict Management: A Framework for analysis', *Review of International Studies*. Vol. 21:359–87.

8   Tar, U.A. (2018). The Ecology of Terrorism: Interrogating the Impact of Armed Conflict on Environmental Security in North Eastern, Nigeria. Lead Paper Presented at the National Political Science Association (NPSA) Conference, held on the 23rd – 25th April, 2018 at the Federal University Kashere, Gombe State.

Radicalisation Theory

This developed from an assumption that individuals who hold extreme views that are away from "moderate mainstream beliefs" are radicals.[9] Hence, the theory adopts an indicator-based approach, which aims to identify persons who are probable, to engage in political and/or religious motivated violence. The indicators in radicalisation theory focuses on push and pull factors that attract individuals to violence. Push factors are personal reasons pushing individuals to radical ideologies while pull factors attract individuals that are potential terrorists [10] and includes narratives that give answers to (negative) push factors.[11]

On one hand, push factors are characterised by identity crisis (internal) that leads folks to hold extremist ideologies and subsequent radicalisation.[12] On the contrary, pull factors are associated with social networks (external), which are interlinked to activation of radical ideas and extreme ideologies within individuals.[13] These networks imply both online and offline interactions. These factors include perceived oppression of Muslims worldwide, strong conviction to support jihad as part of their religious and ideological duty, desire to change the world and build a new state.[14] Pull factors may include the glamour associated with the jihad war, which is perceived to have a cause [15] Radicalisation theory entails "individuals

---

9   Monaghan, J., & Molnar, A. (2016). Radicalisation theories, policing practices, and "the future of terrorism?".*Critical Studies on Terrorism*, 9(3), pp.393-413.

10 Borum, R. (2011). "Rethinking Radicalization." *Journal of Strategic Security.* 4 (4), p. 37–62.

11 Wiktorowicz, Q. (2004). *Suicide Bombings: Do Beliefs Matter?* University of North Carolina.

12 Filoramo, G. (2003). "Religious Pluralism and Crises of Identity." Diogenes 50 (3): 31–44. Doi: 10.1177/ 03921921030503003

13 Segeman, M. (2008).*Leaderless Jihad: Terror Networks in the Twenty-First Century.* Philadelphia: University of Pennsylvania Press; Neumann, P. (2013). "The Trouble with Radicalisation." *International Affairs.* 89 (4): 873–893. doi:10.1111/1468-2346.12049.

14 Saltman, E., & Smith, M. (2015). 'Till Martyrdom Do Us Part': Gender and the ISIS Phenomenon. Institute for Strategic Dialogue; Bakker, E., De Leede, S. and Note, I.B., (2015). European Female Jihadists in Syria: Exploring an Under-Researched Topic. The Hague: International Centre for [Online] https://www.icct.nl/download/file/ ICCT-Bakker-de-Leede-European-Female-Jihadists-In-Syria-Exploring-An-Under-Researched-Topic-April2015 (1). Pdf. (Accessed on 29th August, 2019).

15 Perešin, A. (2015). Fatal Attraction: Western Muslim as and ISIS. *Perspectives on Terrorism*, 9(3).

to join radical collectives, which develops in a real-world location, such as mosques, prisons, shisha bars, sport clubs, and bookshops".[16] Thus, radicalisation theory fits best in guiding the suggestion in this thesis, that a holistic approach to terrorism is essential for interrogating transnational terrorism in the Chad Basin; this will also help in policy programming and initiatives for countering the menace of terrorism.

The criticism of radicalisation theory is that its indicator-based approach easily translates to profiling practices.[17] This is for instance in practice adopted by policing agents.[18] However, radicalisation theorists under the 'narrative school' expand these indicators to a holistic approach whereby, credible indicators are grounded on a wide range of potential and credible variables that are derived from social and political contexts.[19]

Regional Security Complex Theory (RSCT)

This as advanced by Buzan and Wæver[20] is a functionalist perspective on security regionalisation. RSCT offers a theoretical and conceptual framework for understanding the emergent structure and dynamics of international security. It also conceives the historical dynamics and continuities that characterise pre-Cold War (before1945), Cold War (1945–1989/90) and post-Cold War (from1990) global transformations, with implications for regionalism and regionalisation. The concept has constructivist roots emphasising that the evolution of regional security complexes is influenced by patterns of amity and enmity amongst units in the International system.[21]

---

16 Pearson, E. (2015). The Case of Roshonara Choudhry: Implications for Theory on Online Radicalization, ISIS Women, and the Gendered Jihad. Policy & Internet.

17 Monaghan, J., & Molnar, A. (2016). Radicalisation theories, policing practices, and "the future of terrorism?".*Critical Studies on Terrorism*, 9(3), pp.393-413.

18 Breen-Smyth, M. (2014)."Theorising the "Suspect Community": Counter terrorism, Security Practices and the Public Imagination." *Critical Studies on Terrorism.* 7 (2), p. 223–240; Stuart Croft (2012), "Securitizing Islam: Identity and the Search for Security". Cambridge: Cambridge University Press; Kundnani, A. (2014). "Radicalisation: The Journey of a Concept". In Counter Radicalisation: Critical Perspectives, edited by C. Heath-Kelly, L. Jarvis and C. Baker-Beall. Hoboken, NJ: Taylor and Francis

19 Bramadat, P., and L. Dawson, (2014) (Eds).*Religious Radicalization and Securitization in Canada and Beyond.* Toronto: University of Toronto Press.

20 Buzan,B. and Wæver,O. (2003). *Regions and Powers: The Structure of International Security.* Cambridge: Cambridge University Press.

21 Ibid

The realities of conflict and co-operation are dependent on the actions and perceptions of actors as well as power equations.

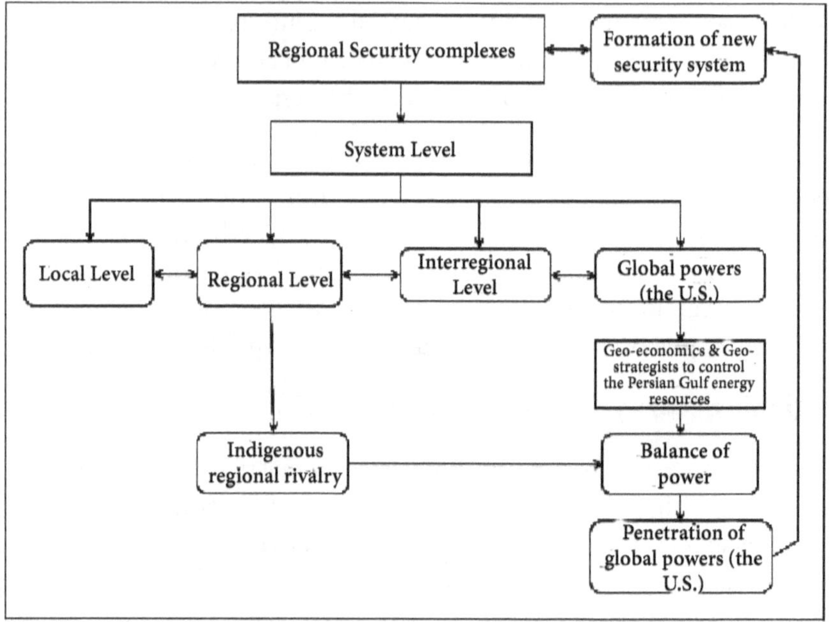

Figure I: Regional Security Complex Model

Source: www.google.com

RSCT was developed to increase the frontiers of knowledge on the interplay of middle level security relations between two extremes–national and global securities. First, the theory views national securities as interconnected, rather than isolated phenomena. They are inter-connected yet emphasise the Nation as the subject and object of security. This is captured in Buzan's pioneering definition of a security complex, defined as 'a group of states whose security concerns link them together sufficiently closely, that their national securities cannot reasonably be considered apart from one another'.[22] Second, the theory views global security as normative, aspirational and often illusive. This is because global security is hinged on the architecture of international law and order, which, unlike municipal or regional order, is difficult to enforce and adjudicate. The third realm is regional security, which is seen as realistic in the sense that it provides a space where security

---

22 Buzan,B. (1991).*People, States and Fear: An Agenda for International Security Studies in the Post-Cold War Era*. England: Pearson, pp.187

units (states) come together, where the two 'extremes of national and global, interplay'.[23] A 'Regional Security Complex', is thus, defined as: 'a set of units whose major process of securitisation, (de) securitisation or both are so interlinked, that their security problems cannot reasonably be analysed or resolved apart from one another'.[24]

Mapping the Dynamics of Transnational Terrorism in the Lake Chad Basin

Boko Haram was established by an Islamic preacher called Mohammed Yusuf, who rose to prominence out of a renewed discussion on the role of Islam in Northern Nigeria in the early 2000's. He assumed leadership of a Salafi group in the city of Maiduguri, where he established a religious community centre (*Markaz*) with a mosque, micro-finance schemes, and farms. The group allegedly had the name Ahlul sunna wal'jama'ah hija (Followers of the Teachings of the Prophet and his Community), but it eventually became known as Boko Haram. Mohammed Yusuf was known for vigorously preaching against what he saw as the eroding effects of Western influence on northern Nigerian Islamic communities and culture – he used the word 'boko' to denote this effect.[25]

In the year 2003-2004, a group known as the Nigerian Taliban comprising people linked with Yusuf, tried to establish a semi-secessionist community in the village of Kanama, Yusuf's birthplace. They were allegedly dissatisfied with Yusuf's slow approach of building a community and focus on preaching (*Da'wah*) over violent confrontation. The group had clashed with security forces, and its members were either killed or dispersed. The increased attention compelled Yusuf to go into exile in Saudi Arabia, from where he returned and continued to develop his Markaz amongst the wider community. When the police shot and wounded several of the group's members during a funeral procession in June 2009, a furious Yusuf demanded that the responsible officers be prosecuted. When nothing happened, he told his followers to prepare for war. The following month saw clashes between protesters and security forces in several Northern

23 Buzan,B. and Wæver,O. (2003). *Regions and Powers: The Structure of International Security.* Cambridge: Cambridge University Press, pp.43

24 Ibid, pp.44

25 Mohammed, N.S. (2017). The Niger Delta Avengers, Autonomous Ethnic Clans and Common Claim Over Oil Wells: The Paradox of Resource Control. *African Research Review*, Vol. 11, No 12, pp. 42 55.DOI. http://dx.doi.org/10.4314/afrrev.v11i2.4

Nigerian states. The security forces called in reinforcements, and in the following operation an estimated 800 people, mostly innocent bystanders, were killed. Consequently, Yusuf was arrested, tortured, and executed, something that amplified his followers' pre-existing acrimonies toward the government – this blend of revolutionary resentment and brutality of security forces fundamentally shaped the group's modus operandi through a sense of retaliation, and in speeches, they have consistently referred to Yusuf's killing.[26]

After the violent clampdown, the state professed the group as extinct. However, in September 2010 Boko Haram had conducted a spectacular jailbreak in the state of Bauchi under a new name, *Jama'atul Ahlus-Sunnah Lidda' Awati wal Jihad* (People Committed to the Teachings of the Prophet and Jihad, JAS), under the leadership of Shekau. The group had conducted a campaign of assassinations targeting politicians, police officers, and religious and village leaders, in what can be branded as acts of retaliation against people by whom the group felt betrayed. A few months later, on Christmas Eve, several bombs went off in the central Nigerian town of Jos and in Maiduguri, which showed that the group had larger ambitions than retaliation and that they were willing to use extreme violence to achieve them.[27] In 2011, the group extended its targets with two ambitious operations in the Nigerian capital of Abuja, the first against the Police Headquarters in June and the second against the UN Headquarters in August. The group thereby, demonstrated a level of sophistication, which to some analysts suggested external support possibly gained through establishing links to Al-Qaeda in the Islamic Maghreb (AQIM). The two vehicle-borne Improvised Explosive Devices (IEDs) used were thought, by analysts, to surpass the group's capacities, and none of the group's operations had hitherto suggested the capacity to hit targets as relatively well defended and remote from Boko Haram's North-eastern areas of operation. That Boko Haram had or could develop connections to AQIM had been suspected, since AQIM's then leader in early 2010 offered assistance to Boko Haram. However, Boko Haram's developing ruthlessness became an obstacle in preserving and making new allies. After a coordinated attack on the city of Kano in January 2012, where both Muslims and Christians were targeted, a

---

26 Ibid

27 Dauda, A. (2017). From Sectarianism to Terrorism in Northern Nigeria: A Closer Look at Boko Haram. In Varin, C., and Dauda, A., (Eds.), *Violent Non-State Actors in Africa: Terrorists, Rebels and Warlords*. Palgrave Macmillan.

group calling itself amā'atu Anṣāril Muslimīna fī Bilādis Sūdā (Defenders of Muslims in the Black Lands, Ansaru) announced that it had broken away from Boko Haram, as they were unsatisfied with the group's attacks on Muslims. When Boko Haram in September 2013 had massacred several predominantly Muslim pupils in the city of Gujba, AQIM also cut the bonds with the group and even issued a fatwa (ruling) against the group.[28]

In May 2013, the Nigerian State had declared a state of emergency in four Northeast-Nigerian states and initiated a 'Grand Military Operation' against Boko Haram. Boko Haram was put under significant pressure and driven from its urban centres of operation. Through personal networks and a terrorism campaign of intimidation of local communities, the group managed to gain a foothold in rural Borno and the surrounding region. The group's brutal methods affected its popular support negatively, but at the same time, a parallel campaign of violence arbitrated by Nigerian security forces, which included arbitrary arrests, extrajudicial executions, and widespread excesses and violations allowed the group to maintain a local support base or resulted in locals not trusting or supporting security forces. Security forces accounted for three fourths of all violent deaths in Boko Haram affected areas in 2013 – the insurgency-terrorism inflicted by Boko Haram was reciprocated with state-terrorism, creating a toxic dialectic of violence against the civilian population.[29]

The year 2015 began with Boko Haram's largest massacre to date in the town of Baga, which is situated on the shores of Lake Chad, and is a garrison town for the Multinational Joint Task Force (MJTF) consisting of soldiers from Niger, Chad, Cameroon, and Nigeria. When Boko Haram had come to the town in January 2015, its residents had assisted the soldiers in trying to repel the attack. After routing the soldiers, Boko Haram took gruesome revenge on the residents – as many as 2,000 people were massacred. Subsequently, the group had released two videos – one of the videos featured the group's leader Shekau, who had taunted the Nigerian army while he showed captured weaponry and took responsibility for killing the town's' 'infidels'. In the other video a hitherto unknown person was seen portraying the massacre as self-defence, inviting all Muslims

28 Onuoha, F.C. (2012). From Ahlulsunna wal'jama'ah hijra to Jama'atu Ahlissunnah lidda'awati wal Jihad. *Africa Insight*. Vol. 41(4):159 - 175.

29 Hansen, W. (2017). Boko Haram: Religious Radicalism and Insurrection in Northern Nigeria. *Journal of Asian and African Studies*. Vol. 52(4): 551 - 569.

to move to the conquered territory, and ending the video by burning a Nigerian flag. The massacre in Baga could be viewed as a reaction to the significant defeats the group had suffered in the prior weeks. The Nigerian army and supporting forces from the MJTF were gaining momentum with the help from local hunters with a tradition for fighting cattle rustlers and road bandits, who had organised self-defence groups, and a private military firm named Specialized Task, Training, Equipment and Protection, which had been contracted by the state.[30]

Concurrently with experiencing setbacks, the group swore allegiance to a (at the time) new player on the Global Jihadi scene: The Islamic State of Syria and the Levant (ISIL, later Islamic State, IS). IS had proclaimed a territorial caliphate from the city of Mosul in June 2014. In March 2015, Boko Haram was praised in the IS magazine Dabiq, where they were referred to by the name Al-Wilāyat -Al-Islāmiyya Gharb Afrīqiyyah (Islamic State's West African Province, ISWAP). After swearing allegiance, Boko Haram had experienced a temporary success – the alliance was manifested in the group's propaganda videos. However, Boko Haram never could manage to exploit the initial success and regain the offensive, losing significant parts of their territory throughout 2015.[31] On 16 January 2017, Boko Haram had again showed their continued capacity for violence, when three suicide bombers detonated themselves at the University of Maiduguri, killing one professor and wounding 17 students. Among the attackers was a 12-year-old girl.[32] The presence of young girls and women in Boko Haram suicide attacks, although rare in conflicts in general, has become a hallmark for the group. Suicide attacks have been effectively used by the group to put pressure on security forces, undermine and challenge the legitimacy and authority of the state, intimidate and exhaust the local population, show initiative when on the defensive, and maintain a presence in urban centres, as the attacks in 2017 illustrate. It is also a reminder that even if the group is defeated militarily, it will not necessarily mean a complete

---

30 Cocodia, J. (2017). Nationalist Sentiment, Terrorist Incursions and the Survival of the Malian State. In Varin, C., & Abubakar, D., (eds.). *Violent Non-State Actors in Africa*. U.S.A.: Palgrave Macmillan.

31 Gray, P., and Adeakin, I. (2015). The Evolution of Boko Haram: From Missionary Activism to Transnational Jihad and the Failure of the Nigerian Security Intelligence Agencies. *African Security*. Vol. 8(3):185-211, 2015.

32 Vanguard (2017). Prof Killed in Maiduguri Suicide Bomb Attack Identified. Vanguard, 16th January, 2017. Retrieved: https://www.vanguardngr.com/news. (Accessed on 6th August, 2019).

end to the violence – the group will likely retract to the local communities from where they came and form underground terror cells – ruthlessness and flexibility have concurrently been Boko Haram's biggest strength and weakness. Their willingness to exploit taboos and break social norms, use indiscriminate violence and adopt a wide range of tactics to out manoeuvre security forces, checkpoints, and local vigilantes manning markets etc., has been a key to their successful operations.

Boko Haram has been able to take advantage of networks of affiliates throughout the region. Northeast Nigeria is part of the old Kanem-Bornu Empire that stretched across Chad, parts of Niger, Cameroon, and Libya. The ethnic majority in these areas is the Kanuri, who are said to have made up the majority of Boko Haram members. Boko Haram has been able to exploit such linguistic, cultural, religious, and kinship relationships to create networks across the region. In addition, high-ranking members such as Mamman Nur, who is from Cameroon, or Khalid al-Barnawi, who allegedly smuggled cigarettes and cocaine with AQIM commander Mokhtar Belmokhtar, have had existing networks across the region and continent.[33]

Between 2009 crackdown and 2010 resurfacing of Boko Haram, Nur went to Somalia to train with al-Shabab and Khalid al-Barnawi in Algeria and to train with AQIM. Shekau has, together with other members, had allegedly used Mali as a sanctuary. It is uncertain how many of these connections are still intact, as well as what new connections Boko Haram has established throughout the African continent. Some sources state that the group has contacts to cells in the Senegal as well as to Séléka rebels in the Central African Republic. Others state that it has recently reached out to the Allied Defense Force in the Democratic Republic of Congo. Thus, it is feared that the group could re-mobilise or seek to plug-in to other conflicts in the region. In the near future, the ability to establish regional collaboration to dismantle the terror or insurgency networks will be decisive in terms of developing sustainable security solutions in the region.[34]

---

33 Gourley, S.M. (2012). Linkages Between Boko Haram and al Qaeda: A Potential Deadly Synergy. *Global Security Studies*. Vol. 3(3): 1 - 14.

34 Ibid; Gray, P., and Adeakin, I. (2015). The Evolution of Boko Haram: From Missionary Activism to Transnational Jihad and the Failure of the Nigerian Security Intelligence Agencies. *African Security*. Vol. 8(3).185-211, 2015

Throughout Boko Haram's existence, it has been more or less unclear what its main objective is. This has made it very difficult to initiate negotiations with the group, in contrast to the Niger Delta Militants. They had very specific objectives, which basically came down to wanting a piece of the cake in light of the endemic exploitation of local oil resources and consequent destruction of the natural environment, traditionally sustaining the communities. They were, therefore, possible to co-opt with money and job opportunities. Boko Haram's sporadic remarks about fighting to establish Sharia in Nigeria and the rest of the world do not provide a clear foundation for negotiations.[35]

Cross border infiltrations of insurgents into Chad prompted N'djamena to join regional collaboration to fight the insurgents. Chad then launched intervention into Northern Cameroon, after the signing of a bilateral agreement, with the intention of clearing its provinces of Boko Haram fighters and camps, and re-securing the supply routes of the militant and curtailed further weaponisation of the region. Thus, the Chadian army initiated a unilateral offensive to dislodge the insurgents from their Nigerian territories. This was followed by a Nigerian offensive in the same area, while the Nigerien Military launched a campaign in the Diffa region in South-eastern Niger to push back insurgent units operating there.[36]

The BHTs group had transformed from being a local terrorist organisation, by pledging allegiance to Islamic ISIS on 7th March 2015, which was subsequently accepted by the leadership of the ISIS on 13th March 2015. They claimed to have established an Islamic State in West Africa (ISWA) comprising of the 4th Region of Cameroun and 4th region of Chad in Central Africa as well as 5th region of Niger and North-eastern parts of Nigeria in West Africa. These areas form the major parts of the MNJTF area of operational responsibility.[37] Having analysed the evolution of BHT to aid the understanding of the region's security dilemma, the next section will unpack the emerging regional security architecture in the LCB.

---

35 Maiangwa, J.S., & Audu, A.R. (2017). Civilians in Frontlines: Evolving Grassroots Force for Counter-Insurgency Operations in the Lake Chad Basin Region. In Tar, U. A., (ed.), *Defence Transformation and the Consolidation of Democracy in Nigeria*. Kaduna-Nigeria: Nigerian Defence Academy Press.

36 Nasrulallah, F. (2015).The expanding War in the Lake Chad. Retrieved: http://fulanisitrep.com/2015/11/19/the-expanding-war-in-the-lake-chad. (Accessed on 21st August, 2019).

37 Ibid

The Response: Emerging Regional Security Architecture in the Lake Chad Basin

The New World (dis) Order has resulted in the relative neglect of conflicts in the global South.[38] Following the United Nations Security Council's demand for robust transnational and regional counter terrorism measures,[39] states in the region have increasingly been impelled to act collectively. Against the backdrop of emerging security realities, states within the LCBC had decided to form a far-reaching generic transnational counter terrorism measure, with the expansion of the mandate of the MNJTF in the LCB. The MNJTF reflects a regional military alliance to coordinate efforts to combat the common threats to their national security posed by the Islamic fundamentalist group. This security architecture, under the ambit of 'international border control' to 'counter terrorism', is driven by the changing dynamics of conflict in Africa, in particular the resurgence of violent Islamist terrorism, and the geopolitics of regional powers. Reminiscence of the West African security regionalism underpinning ECOMOG in the 1990s, the MNJTF in the LCBC represents a new security frontier. The MNJTF is a platform for African-led multilateral.

In the LCB, the geostrategic implications of Boko Haram insurgency have altered the power configuration.[40] This has called for the necessary deployment of a security regimen. As a result of the frequency of security threats posed by BH, in the LCB, there is undergoing the emergence of a new security order and regional configuration. As a regional power, Nigeria and its neighbours in the region had realised the tremendous negative geostrategic consequences of Boko Haram's transnational border attacks and demanded for the supply of collective regional security arrangements to decimate the insurgency and other criminalities.[41]

38 Schulz, Michael/Söderbaum, Fredrik/Öjendal, Joakim (eds) (2001) Regionalization in a Globalizing World. A Comparative Perspective on Actors, Forms and Processes, London: Zed Books, pp.67

39 Heupel,M. (2007).'Adapting to Transnational Terrorism: The UN Security Council's Evolving Approach to Terrorism', *Security Dialogue*38 (4):477–99

40 Tar, U.A., & Mustapha, M. (2016).Emerging Architecture of Regional Security Complex in the Lake Chad Basin. Being a Paper Presented at the *International Conference on Security Regimens in Africa* Organised by CODESERIA, Held at Azalai Grand Hotel, Bamako, Mali, 28 – 29 September.

41 Tar, U.A., & Bala, B. (2019). Terrorism, Insurgency and the Challenges of Counter-Terrorism and Counter-Insurgency. In Tar, U.A., & Bala, B., (eds), *New Architecture for Regional Security in Africa: Perspectives on Counter-Terrorism and Counter-Insurgency in the Lake Chad Basin*. Lanham, MD: Lexington Books.

Against the backdrop, of emerging security realities, states within the LCBC had decided to form far-reaching generic transnational counter terrorism measures. Further, there was expansion of the mandate of the Multinational Joint Task Force (MNJTF) in the Lake Chad Basin as a security mechanism, representing the emerging space for sub-regional securitisation and a regional response to the challenges of violent terrorism.

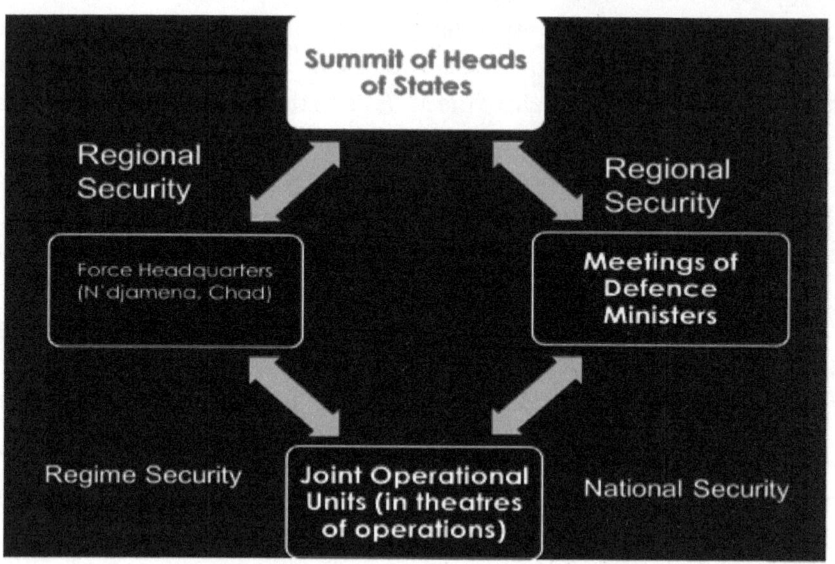

Figure II: Lake Chad Basin Security Architecture

Source: The Author

MNJTF reflects a regional military alliance, to coordinate efforts to combat the common threat to national and collective regional security, posed by the Islamic fundamentalist terrorist group. This emerging regional security architecture institutionalised a paradigm shift and change of mandate of the MNJTF from 'international border control' (1990s) to 'counter terrorism' outfit (2015+). MNJTF as a platform for African-led multilateral securitisation and counter terrorism has focused solely on inter-states security dialogue, bringing together the regional defence Chiefs to coordinate region wide counter-terrorism measures. Increased threats by Islamic radicalism have led to integration of counter-terrorism into LCBC emerging regional security agenda.[42]

---

42 This Day Newspaper (2015). UN Security Council demands Boko Haram end all violence in Lake Chad Bain. 2015. Retrieved: http://www.thisdaylive.com. (Accessed on

In January 2014, the four countries revisited the MNJTF, originally formed in 1998, to deal with the cross-border security issues and extend its mandate to conduct joint military operations against Boko Haram in the Lake Chad region. At its 14th summit of Heads of State and Government, held in Chad in April 2012, the LCBC had decided to reactivate the force and extend its mandate and operational frontier to include containing the growing regional threats of Boko Haram. The headquarters of that force previously located in the city of Baga in Nigeria's Borno State, had fallen in the hands of Boko Haram in 2015.[43]

At the continental level, the MNJTF as regional military coalition to fight Africa's jihadists in the Lake Chad region was endorsed by the AU PSC during its Assembly Summit held on 29th January 2015 in Addis Ababa. The draft concept of operations (CONOPS) for the operationalisation of the MNJTF was reviewed by the PSC on 03 March 2015. Member countries of the LCBC were mandated to mobilize forces to fight the terrorist group, which has increased the spate of its attacks in Cameroon, Chad and Niger. As a follow-up to its decision of 29 January 2015, the PSC held a session on the steps being taken for the operationalization of the MNJTF against Boko Haram by the Lake Chad Basin Countries LCBC and Benin.[44]

The AU's authorisation of the MNJTF was requested by member states of the Lake Chad Basin Commission LCBC– Cameroon, Chad, Niger, and Nigeria–as well as by a non-member state, Benin, after a ministerial meeting in Niamey, Niger. It was agreed that the 8,700-strong force headquartered in N'Djamena, Chad, would be authorised to exercise a "right of hot pursuit" on Nigerian soil. The LCBC members states agreed that harmonizing on a concept of operations, is a crucial step in obtaining the United Nations' (UN) legitimisation–and perhaps funding–for the MNJTF through a UN Security Council Resolution. At a meeting held in Yaoundé, Cameroon, on 5–7 February 2015, experts from the Lake Chad Basin Commission and the AU, with the participation of experts from the Economic Community of West African States (ECOWAS), the European Union and the UN, formally finalized the draft operational plans. The plan

---

23rd August, 2019).

43 Yoroms, G.J. (2016). 'Counter terrorism Measures in West Africa' in Wofula O and Annedi B (eds), *Understanding Terrorism in Africa: Building Bridges and Overcoming the Gaps,* Institute of Security Studies, Pretoria.

44 Ibid

outlined the strategic coordination, rules of engagement, and requirements for supporting and sustaining the mission.[45]

MNJTF's Strategy - In line with the decisions by the LCBC Member States, the MNJTF's mission is to operate with the AU PSC authority to eliminate BHTs, to create a safe and secure environment and facilitate the stabilization in the areas by using all the necessary means with its capacity. In order to create a safe-secure environment and contribute to stabilizing the situation in the affected areas, and using all necessary conventional means within its capacity and with the support of relevant bilateral partners as well as regional and international organisations, the MNJTF does the following:[46]

(a) Carries on and execute security operations to regain full control of the areas under BH threat and occupation.

(b) Support the member countries of the LCBC to effectively exercise and maintain State Authority in the areas affected by the activities of BH and other bandit groups and provide protection to the civilian population under immediate threat.[47]

(c) On the other hand, the strategic end state of the MNJTF is to ensure that the presence and influence of BHTs is completely eliminated. The security conditions are to be re-established for the states exercising full authority over the areas affected by the activities, and assuming their responsibilities for the protection of the population, properties and livelihood means, as well as for addressing regional security and human rights challenges. Operational cooperation is adequately enhanced in the region and the LCBC Member States can implement the overall stabilization programs in the affected areas.

---

45 Théroux-Bénoni, L.A. (2015).'The Fight against Boko Haram Tangled up in Nigerian and Regional Politics', Institute for Security Studies, https://www.issafrica.org/iss-today/the-fight-against-boko-haram-tangled-up-in-nigerian-and-regional-politics.

46 Yoroms, G.J. (2016). 'Counter terrorism Measures in West Africa' in Wofula O and Annedi B (eds), *Understanding Terrorism in Africa: Building Bridges and Overcoming the Gaps,* Institute of Security Studies, Pretoria; Agbor T.I.,& Abdullahi L.F. (2017). 'Taming the Monster: Boko Haram' in Mohammed M and Abdullahi LF, (Eds), *Global Terrorism: The Nigerian Experience in Taming Boko Haram,* Lagos, Nigeria

47 Agbor T.I.,& Abdullahi L.F. (2017). 'Taming the Monster: Boko Haram' in Mohammed M and Abdullahi LF, (Eds), *Global Terrorism: The Nigerian Experience in Taming Boko Haram,* Lagos, Nigeria

MNJTF's Mandate - Within the framework of its mandate and in its Area of Operation (AO), the MNJTF is to carry out the following tasks among others:

(a) Conduct security operations to prevent the expansion of BH and other terrorists' group activities and eliminate their presence.

(b) Facilitate operational coordination amongst the TCCs, LCBC member states, Benin and other stakeholders in the fight against BH and other terrorist groups, based on the intelligence collected as well as from other relevant African structures availed by partners.

(c) Conduct patrols and other types of operations in the area of operation.

(d) Conduct operations to disrupt the supply lines of BHTs and other terrorist groups, preventing the transfer of arms and ammunition and other type of support.

(e) Ensure, upon request and within the means and capabilities of the MNJTF, the protection of civilians under immediate threat, IDP and refugee camps, humanitarian workers and other civilian personnel.

(f) Actively search for, and free all abductees, including the young girls abducted in Chibok town of Nigeria in April 2014.

The draft concept also outlines the establishment of a Central Military Command and joint coordination mechanism that will have control over troops contributed by LCBC members and Benin. A Force Commander rotating among LCBC members and Benin will hold the Operational Command and control of the force. Although the AU's decision was to have MNJTF's force size of 7,500, however, during the Yaoundé meeting representatives of Benin, Cameroon, Chad, Niger and Nigeria, Nigeria announced that they wished to increase the size by 1,200 personnel. Nigeria is the largest contributor with 3,250 personnel, followed by Chad with 3,000.[48]

---

48 Agbor T.I.,& Abdullahi L.F. (2017). 'Taming the Monster: Boko Haram' in Mohammed M and Abdullahi LF, (Eds), *Global Terrorism: The Nigerian Experience in Taming Boko Haram*, Lagos, Nigeria

The MNJTF Command and Control Framework - The MNJTF Command Structure at strategic, operational and tactical levels are structured in a hierarchical format. First, at the strategic level, the LCBC in close coordination with the AU Commission serves as the Strategic Headquarters for the MNJTF. Secondly, at the operational level, the Operational Headquarters of the MNJTF is established in N'djamena, Chad and is staffed by Personnel from LCBC Member States and Benin. It also comprises relevant bilateral and international partners, particularly from the P3 (USA, UK and France) through the Centre for Coordination and Liaison (CCL). The MNJTF HQs and their military and civilian staff operate under the authority of the MNJTF Commander. At the tactical level, the MNJTF ground forces comprise of national contingents pledged from the countries affected by Boko Haram and other terrorist groups. The Forces comprise tactical combat units and other units deemed necessary. The MNJTF HQ facilitates the conduct of joint, simultaneous and coordinated patrols and other types of operations. The three levels structure of the MNJTF is to ensure that each level provide the relevant support to ensure mission success.[49]

The MNJTF Operations - The MNJTF operations are premised on the various compositions of troops pledged by the TCCs. These include motorized and mechanized battalions, gendarmerie, engineers, amphibious elements, artillery and other support elements. The entire operations are conducted in five phases.

(a) **Common to all Phases**: This is the generic phase under which the MNJTF forces maintain a reserve capability (up to a battalion size); secure the logistical LOCs; ensure permanent Force security measures; collect intelligence throughout the AoO; establish liaison with all actors and at all levels (including national security and defence forces - SDF, partner NGOs, IOs and UN Agencies); and maintain the MNJTF headquarters at N'Djamena.

(b) **Planning for Deployment**: This encompasses conduct of planning activities (CONOPS Development); force generation; reconnaissance missions to potential future deployment sites; force preparation of units on standby to be ready for deployment;

---

49 Yoroms, G.J. (2016). 'Counter terrorism Measures in West Africa' in Wofula O and Annedi B (eds), *Understanding Terrorism in Africa: Building Bridges and Overcoming the Gaps,* Institute of Security Studies, Pretoria.

deployment of the Sector HQs; integration of forces deployed and operating in the AoO; build-up of the logistical support arrangements; commencement of a public information and communication campaign; and mapping of refugees' camps and IDP sites

(c) **Deployment**: Under this phase, troops are deployed on combat missions to the various targets in the AoO. Specifically, this phase involves control by each force component of its dedicated Area of operations; seize and control of key areas in the AoO; secure mobility corridors and main locations with significant population density; consolidation of strongholds; support to CIMIC and other psychological operations; and preparation of operations.

(d) **Conduct Offensive Operations**: This phase involves the conduct of specific, target offensive missions with emphasis on the following: isolate and neutralize BH factions; disorganize C2 and communications systems; disrupt supply lines; disorganize smuggling networks; reduce military capability; clear hideouts and training centres; protect most vulnerable populations; facilitate, upon request, the delivery of humanitarian assistance even under fire; neutralize logistical support bases; conduct stop and search operations to capture key BH leaders; search for and free all persons abducted and provide security to refugee camps, as feasible

(e) **Stabilisation:** This phase involves the provisions of stabilisation operations and services to the civil population. It involves the following: reduce isolated resistance elements; search BH hideouts; facilitate the return of IDPs and Refugees; support the re-establishment of state authority in areas freed from BH occupation; support the implementation of actions towards the enhancement of public order in the concerned areas; promote delivery of the social fabric; and contribute to the initial steps of a Demobilization, Disarmament and Reintegration (DDR) process.

(f) **Force Drawdown:** This is the forecast phase that involves preparedness for ending the mission. This involves the following: reassessment of the security situation in the AoO; readjust the deployment of units on the ground; redeployment as necessary; rotation if necessary; dismantling of logistical support arrangements; IOT reaction to any attack by BH.

Prospect and Challenges: There are both incentives and challenges that underpin the emerging regional security complex in the LBC. Despite its limitations in terms of funding, the MNJTF has thus, far managed some success against Boko Haram. In February and March 2014, the armies of the MNJTF had recaptured 36 towns across three states in the North-east of Nigeria. Forces from Chad and Niger were instrumental in expelling Boko Haram from the key towns of Mallam Fatori and Damasak, killing 300 fighters in the process. It is pertinent to note that, the emergence of Buhari as new Nigeria's President in May 2015, has further enhanced the momentum and the political will for a broader regional response to combat Boko Haram. The Nigerian President had made ending the Boko Haram insurgency, a key point of his electoral campaign, and shortly after assuming office, had begun reforming his command structure, appointing new Military Service Chiefs, and moving counter terrorism centre of operations to Maiduguri, the epicentre of the insurgency and increase regional cooperation with its neighbours Cameroon, Chad, and Niger. In a separate but equally momentous bilateral agreement, Nigeria had agreed to allow Chadian troops to enter Nigerian territory to fight Boko Haram, under the right of "hot pursuit" across its borders.[50]

The challenges confronting the emerging regional counter terrorism response in the LCB include among others, historical contradictions, linguistic differences, resources, geopolitics, hegemonic politics, and local national politics have also hampered meaningful progress and undermined the basis for erecting robust new security architecture in the region.[51]

Conclusion

This paper has examined the Trans-nationalization of terrorism in the Lake Chad Basin and emerging regional counter terrorism responses. This transformation of the world into a 'Global Village' through the use of

---

50 Daily Post Newspaper (2016), 'Boko Haram: FG Signs MoU on Citing of MNJTF Intelligence Headquarters in Abuja'. Available at http://dailypost.ng. (Accessed on 23rd August, 2019); Oputu,D.and Lilley,K. (2015).'Boko Haram and Escalating Regional Terror', http://soufangroup.com/tsg-intelbrief-boko-haram-and-escalating-regional- terror.

51 Tar, U.A. & Bala, B. (2018). Boko Haram Insurgency, Terrorism and the Challenges of Peace building in the Lake Chad Basin. In Omeje, K.C. (Ed.). *Peace building in Contemporary Africa: In Search of Alternative Strategies.* London: Routledge

the internet may well explain the escalation of transnational terrorism in many parts of the world, particularly in the Lake Chad Basin. This is so, as globalization challenges individual state's capacity to manage economic affairs, as well as serving as a facilitator and force multiplier for terrorist organisations. Similarly, globalisation has enabled terrorist groups to develop transnational social capital, create alliances and generate support outside their immediate area of operations.

Thus, the Chad Basin is fast emerging as a new security complex in terms of the broad attributes identified.[52] In addition to sharing the Lake and its resources, countries of the Chad Basin demonstrate several factors in common, like proximate geography, political problems, socio-cultural linkages, economic resources and shared threats to national and regional security. Furthermore, emerging trends suggest that Nigeria, the region's preponderant power - has been brokering the support of countries to put in place new regional security architecture – MNJTF, under the aegis of the LCBC. Headquartered in N'Djamena, Republic of Chad, the Task forces has so far worked hard to confront the threat posed by Boko Haram, albeit with modest success.

Nevertheless, regional geopolitics and the rough terrain of the Chad Basin pose a herculean task for the member states of the Chad Basin Commission. The Chad Basin, however, has proved to be a viable regional security complex in the making. But there are challenges to be overcome in nurturing the Chad Basin regional security complex.

---

52 Buzan,B. and Wæver,O. (2003). *Regions and Powers: The Structure of International Security*. Cambridge: Cambridge University Press.

4

Evolving Challenges of Radicalisation in South Asia

Mr Shafqat Munir

South Asia is a reservoir of human resource and has the highest economic growth in the world with an estimated growth rate of 7.1 percent in 2020 and 2021. South Asia comprises 3.8 percent of the global economy, of which India contributes 3.36 percent. This region is a democratic powerhouse of the world with collective population of 1.81 billion, approximately 3 percent geography of the world. The region has seen approximately 3249 terror related incidents that have led to loss of 5829 lives including civilians and security personals. Notwithstanding, the rise of South Asia economically, the region had a profound impact on the economy due to escalation in terror incidents. One of the main reasons for the spike in violent extremism is radicalisation. According to UNODC, 2012, radicalisation refers primarily to the process of indoctrination that often accompanies the transformation of recruits into individuals determined to act with violence based on extremist ideologies. Radicalisation is a process of indoctrination and transformation of an individual over a period of time, but the question remains, is radicalisation synonymous with terrorism? There is no universally accepted or agreed definition of terrorism but most appropriate to the contemporary situation is, 'Terrorism is the use or threat or use of violence by non-state actors to instil fear in a specified target, which includes innocent civilians.' Radicalisation is not always related to terrorism but more often it is related to violent extremism against citizens with a view to impose a political ideology that may be contrary to the democratic governance.

Terrorism and Radicalisation a Challenge to South Asia

The scourge of terrorism in South Asia is predominantly Islamic, ethno-nationalistic and Left-Wing Extremism. Terrorism gets impetus from radicalisation and new trends that are unfolding, suggest that it is at both, individual and social levels where Individuals are radicalised by social media, religious motivation and quest for martyrdom/ glamorisation of Jihadists. There is also a sense of adventure and perceived duty as a religious solider. At social level, radicalisation is predominantly, due to social exclusion on economic, political and social fronts and second most important reason is family and peer pressure. In Sri Lanka, Easter bombing highlighted that a self-radicalised family acted as a module with no outside linkages.

South Asia is facing the scourge of terrorism since the 60s. Many regional countries are now facing Islamic terrorism and it has a profound impact on the stability of the region. India, Bangladesh and many other countries have faced security challenges from the radicals and violent extremists. The Dhaka bakery terror attack has shown that no section of the society is excluded from the traction of radicalisation. In the Dhaka bakery terror attack, youths from affluent and upper social strata were the main perpetrators. The connection between terrorists and diaspora is not a recent phenomenon. The numbers of people who have gone from Bangladesh to Syria are far less as compared to the overall population. But there are a number of Bangladeshi citizens in Europe and few other countries of West Asia which has been a cause of concern. The reasons could be financial lifeline, access to weapons and international lobbying by diaspora groups. Throughout the 20th century, the Irish Republican Army (IRA) had enjoyed close links with the Irish American community that had supported the IRA to continue with their armed resistance. We are living in an era where lone wolf attacks are emerging at regular intervals. Lone Wolves could be inspired by radical ideology, but not necessarily directed by the ISIS or Al Qaeda and other groups. The principal motivation is a perception of 'Act alone for collective cause' and is often carried out by those who are self-radicalized. The case of 25-years-old Bangladeshi home stay guest student stabbing the owner was an outcome of self-radicalisation. This is an example of self-radicalisation through social media. While women turning into terrorists are more or less unheard of in South Asia, there have been incidents of them turning into radicals and even acting as lone wolves.

According to UNODC, there is a rising trend of radicalisation of women for terror networks. This allows radical organisations to conceal identity more so because women are not associated with violence and extremism in South Asia. Revenge, restoration, relationship, false notion of dignity and respect in social circle are some of the reasons that are the driving force behind female radicalisation. Security forces consider the social image and norms where women are often underestimated when it comes to acts of terror by women. Another looming threat is returning of the foreign fighters. There is a legal lacuna where an act of terror committed in a foreign country is not punishable in their home states. The foreign fighters are passing the know how to local modules. The threat is now increasing especially, from cadres returning from Afghanistan, Syria and Iraq. Foreign fighters may also choose to radicalise others of their local community in non-violent ways.

In the absence of juvenile prison and isolation from the hardened terrorists and radicals, prison radicalisation is emerging as a major challenge. This is like a contamination and unless radicals are isolated and prevented from interaction, the prison radicalisation will create more hardened extremists. The police and prison administrators are not adequately trained to handle de-radicalisation or anti radicalisation measures. It not only requires de-radicalisation strategy but also effective monitoring.

Key Drivers of Radicalisation and De-Radicalisation Measures

What is the main source of encouragement for radicalisation in South Asia? We have fairly good idea why people of South Asia (though miniscule number) are getting attracted to radicalisation and subsequently, leading to acts of terror, and these are economic, social and even political. There are large numbers of youths that get disaffected with the state due to aspirations not being met, or even at times failure in personal lives. As a result, they want to set the societal malice right by adopting violent extremism. Here, two disturbing trends are a cause of worry, family as terror module and youths attracted to transnational terrorism ideology. Family as terror module makes it difficult to monitor and prevent acts of terror. In most cases the family terror module was exposed post incident. The trend of educated and semi educated youth getting attracted to radical transnational terror ideology is on the rise. This traction is due to religious, political, economic, ideological and at times personal failure. Some of the key drivers of radicalisation are a powerful appealing narrative, disenchantment towards society, misinterpretation of religious texts, reaction to global events, lack of transnational cooperation and identity crisis.

South Asia has its own share of challenges that may not be faced by other developed countries. Some of these are difficult borders, governance challenges with population explosion and resource to population ratio shrinking, unemployment and poverty, socio-political challenges and displacement due to violent and non-violent causes. Some of the other reasons are ethno-religious extremism and the artificially created "other vs. us" narrative. Thus, organisations like AQIS looks to manipulate space, access to sophisticated communications and lack of effective regional cooperation.

The response to radicalisation is not sacrosanct. It is specific to each group or individual. Participation of youth should be seen as part of the solution, to develop counter narratives in collaboration with the youth. It must be aimed to raise awareness, preparedness and platforms where constructive discussions and debates can take place. More probing and research to understand the issue needs to be explored. Therefore, counter terror measures must be preventive rather than reactive. It is imperative to incorporate all the stakeholders around the region and build capacity to identify and understand the early symptoms of radicalisation. There is a need to create an integrated awareness campaign with all stakeholders of the societies, across the region. As also to formulate and develop a strategic approach to deal with radicalisation. The role of funding for terrorism is already a challenge and it will become even more complex as one move to a world dominated by Crypto Currency. Rigid and hard-line approach may be counter-productive; thus, a softer empathetic approach may bear greater result. The counter radicalisation strategy must also focus on sharing of real-time intelligence, seamless interagency coordination, development of the whole of society and whole of government approach, creation of a regional intelligence fusion centre, use of technology in response, and finally, incorporate rehabilitation of de-radicalised youth and individuals.

5

Transnational Terrorism: Emerging Challenges to Southeast Asia

Dr. Naing Swe Oo

Terrorism is not new to Southeast Asia. The activities of a variety of domestic ethno- nationalist and religious militant groups posed one of the most significant challenges to internal stability of many countries across the region.[1]

Regional Security and Terrorism

Southeast Asia region is strategically located between Eastern and Western hemispheres. The multi-sectoral cooperation of Association of South East Asian Nations (ASEAN) Member States in political, economic and cultural sectors has much to contribute to regional security and stability.

There are issues such as border disputes between neighbouring countries, multiple claims to certain islands, illegal border trade, transnational crime, smuggling, interference in internal affairs of other nations and terrorism. According to David C. Rapoport there are four waves of terrorism, which are - anarchist wave, anticolonial wave, new left wave and religious wave.

---

1   The Evolving Threat to Southeast Asia by Peter Chalk, Angel Rabasa, William Rosenau, Rand Publication at https://www.rand.org/pubs/monographs/MG846.html

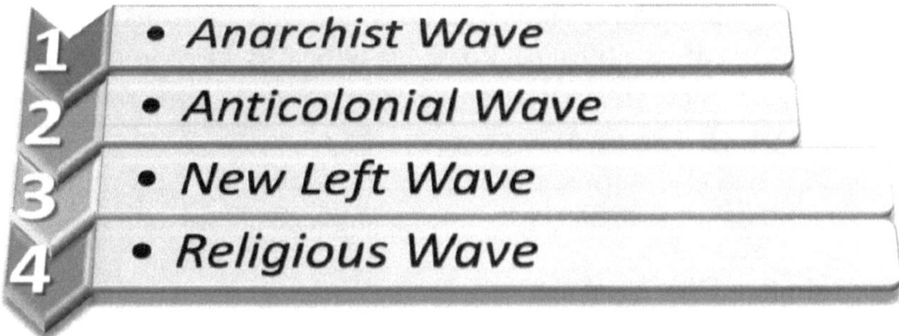

Figure: Waves of Modern Terrorism

The Fifth Wave of Modern Terrorism

There is a concern regarding the emergence of Terrorist Semi States (TSS) in Middle East and North African Region (MENA) and Pakistan, which is creating space for the Fifth Wave. According to *Or Honig & Ido Yahel,* "TSS is super-empowered group that has control over geographic area of a weak state, maintaining governance in controlled territory, while launching terrorist attacks against third-party states".

Regional Security and Terrorism

Southeast Asia has been afflicted by scourge of transnational jihadi terrorism, sometimes subsumed in long-standing insurgencies. The region also has significant problems of poverty and poor governance. These problems enforce spread of terrorism in the region. Southeast Asian states have reaffirmed that terrorism is one of the most serious threats to international peace and security.

Jemaah Islamiyah

Sixteen years after carrying out the Bali bombing, which had killed over 200 people, Al-Qaeda affiliate Jemaah Islamiyah (JI) has remained a key terrorist group in Southeast Asia today. Despite being pushed back since 2009, due to the death of its key leaders and arrest of its members, JI has deep political and ideological roots in the region. The leadership of JI is of the opinion, that they are better organized today and in a state of heightened preparedness. Nasir Abbas is a Malaysian national and former Chief of Training in JI. In 1994, he and Hambali who was responsible for the Bali night club bombing in 2003, travelled to Myanmar via Bangladesh crossing the river between the two countries. Their plan was to set up the terrorist training camp in Rakhine State. When they arrived, they met the leaders of local insurgent group called Rohingya Solidarity Organisation (RSO) a.k.a *Kalarsoe*. They had discussed with them a plan to setup the camps in Rakhine State. But Nasir Abbas gave up the plan because of the difficult terrain. He had also warned the RSO leaders that it will be eliminated by government security forces due to terrain and lack of proxy support.

Islamic State (IS)

There are two Schools of thought about ISIS: some experts are of the view that IS is nearly vanquished as it has failed to hold on to the territory in the Middle East. Second view is, that ISIS is invincible, destined to wreak havoc in Middle East for the next decade and beyond. After losing control over Raqqa, the foreign fighters now have two choices, either return to their native countries, or join other terrorist groups such as Al-Qaeda. However, the returning cadres pose greater challenge to the host nations since each one of them becomes a module that can radicalize and organize cadres within their countries.

Myanmar's Rakhine Case – Security Perspective

Myanmar is a strategic land bridge between South Asia and Southeast Asia. Myanmar is wedged between India and China. It also separates Jihadists operating in South Asia and Al Qaeda affiliates making inroads in South Asia. Myanmar has effectively contained spread of Al Qaeda ideology and is dealing with terror organisations firmly. The terror organisations that Myanmar is confronting are given in succeeding paras.

The Arakan Rohingya Salvation Army (ARSA)

Former name of ARSA was Harakah al-Yaqin (Faith Movement). ARSA is the terrorist extremist group responsible for October 9, 2016 attack and August 25, 2017 attack in Rakhine State. According to Jane's Terrorism & Insurgency Monitor (20 – Jan – 2017), "Rohingya militancy in Myanmar's Rakhine is likely to escalate." The tactics used after October 2016 Attacks are, hit and run, standoff attacks on security posts, small scaled ambushes on foot patrols and convoys, use of Improvised Explosive Devices (IED) and attack on Bengalis suspected informers of security forces. ARSA was able to establish good command and control network. Cadres were well dispersed with adequate support from the network of over ground workers. They had improved their tactics and drills after every attack and had used reinforcements, and interdiction to prevent security forces to reach ambush sites. The only aspect that was conspicuous was the absence of sophisticated weapons and equipment. This could be either by design or lack of availability. In January 2019, ARSA released the paper called 'Reviving the Courageous Hearts', it has 8 Chapters and ARSA emphasized that "ARSA will not stop its resistance movement- both armed and unarmed." According to the International Crisis Group Report, which was published on April 25, 2019, on the conditions of Refugee camps, it stated that "It should also improve law and order in the camps, where militants and gangs increasingly operate with impunity and are consolidating control to the detriment of non-violent political voices and leaders."

The ARSA is now launching armed and unarmed resistance, radicalisation of masses, nonviolent political movement and using criminals, weapon traffickers and smugglers to give impetus to the armed resistance. Trans-regional terror groups can only be contained if there is synergy among the regional countries. ARSA can be dealt with effectively, if Bangladesh too joins to eliminate this threat that may ultimately spread to entire South Asia.

Way Ahead

The government should modernize and strengthen the 'Border Guard Police' to deal with cross border movement of the criminals, terrorists and over ground workers. This may also require incorporating custom and intelligence agencies deployed with Border Guards. Border fencing needs to be completed especially, at critical crossing points. Incorporation of technology is imperative, and deployment of UAVs and drones is a good idea to keep border areas under surveillance. Myanmar could examine various border fences including Israel – Gaza Barrier fence, Indo – Pakistani Border fence and Indo – Bangladeshi Border fence. However, most important is an effective intelligence grid that will enable security forces to do their job professionally.

Conclusion

The peace in Southeast Asia will get disturbed if local Al Qaeda affiliates are allowed to reorganise and establish transnational linkages. It would require synergy and coordination among the intelligence agencies and governments, as well as cooperation to dismantle the network. There is also a need to look within to effectively fight this scourge of terrorism by improving border management, de-radicalisation, use of technology for better surveillance and monitoring of borders day and night.

PART- II

Transnational Terrorism in India's Strategic Neighbourhood

6

Threat of Islamic State of Khorasan in Central Asia: Myth or Reality

Mr Farrukh Juraev

The modern system of international relations has entered a new but difficult period of transformation. New challenges and threats to international and regional security are emerging; this is because of the ongoing wars and conflicts, inter-ethnic and inter-religious contradictions in some parts of the world, as well as the process of migration. The threat of terrorism and extremism are turning into an acute problem for the global community. Today hundreds of terrorist organisations are active across the world. In the last two years, 5000 terrorist attacks have occurred across 70 countries. Terrorist organisations still control significant financial support either through narcotic trade, weapon smuggling or by controlling natural resources. The UN Secretary General Mr. Antonio Guterres had stated that ISIS still has approximately $300 million, even after losing Caliphate. By using modern ICT, extremist groups are actively engaged in recruiting cadres through social media. ISIS has used social media and internet to great advantage and as many as 80 percent of cadres are recruited primarily, through internet, through social networks.

It should be noted that most of the crimes related to violent extremism are committed by people younger than 30 years. According to some estimates, globally there are nearly 300 thousand youths, who are under 18, and are in the religious extremist organisations. Unfortunately, extremist-terrorist propaganda influences youth more than the mature and elderly person. That is why we believe that modern terrorism is a war of minds and hearts of people, especially of the younger generation, and hence, is a decisive factor in dealing with radicalism and terrorism.

In the recent past, the international community has shown increased interest in Central Asia. It is due to the geo-politics, geo-strategic significance, and economic opportunities of the region, that the importance of the region has gone up. In a short period of time a new political reality has been created in Central Asia with the efforts of the President Sh.Mirziyoyev.

Common interest and mutual benefits have become cornerstone of our relationship with the Central Asian countries. Implementation of the principle that "the main priority of Uzbekistan's foreign policy is Central Asia", has contributed to the dual task, with the regional countries, of not only opening borders for free trade and travel, but also markets. Even now, the global community is forging strong trade and cultural ties with the Central Asian nations. On June 22 of 2018, the CAR Nations had adopted a resolution "Strengthening regional and international cooperation to ensure peace, stability and sustainable development in the Central Asian region". The resolution had recognises the role of Central Asian countries in promoting regional and international peace and cooperation. At the same time, it is also important to emphasize that today Central Asian countries are facing serious regional threats from the transnational terrorism. The threat is from rapidly changing situation in the Middle East and North Africa and escalation of geopolitical tensions between global powers. Today, radicalism, extremism and terrorism are posing unprecedented threat to internal security of the states. They penetrate into societal space, institutions of governance and religious organisations, regardless of the level of the civilizational and cultural background. To deal with such a challenge, there is a need to have a multi-pronged approach, including constant dialogue with the citizenry, religious organisations and even inter-governmental agencies. It is imperative to mention that old methods of dealing with rogue agencies and violent extremists do not work now.

International extremists and terrorist organisations are increasingly using information technology and social networking as a tool for recruiting young people. In this regard, it is extremely important to address the root causes of this phenomenon, and not the consequences. Secondly, contain the growing influence of transnational terrorist' organisations, including Islamic State in neighboring Middle East and AF-Pak regions. According to some data, the number of supporters of the ISIS in Afghanistan ranges from two to five thousand people. The share of foreign mercenaries in the composition of the ISIS is 50 percent. According to experts, ISIS is trying to consolidate in Afghanistan, in order to create "Velayat Khorasan". Experts assume that Vilayat Khorasan's expansion in Iran and AF-Pak region will cause instability even in CAR. Thirdly, the armed conflict, has been going on for the last 40 years in Afghanistan and the Republic of Uzbekistan had supported the efforts of the Afghan government and the international community to restore and end the armed struggle. In this context, Uzbekistan has stressed the need to intensify the dialogue, and consider trade, economic, cultural and humanitarian cooperation as the most effective factor in the conflict resolution. We believe that peace and stability in Afghanistan is a strategic necessity for the countries of the region, hence should work towards the peaceful resolution of the conflict. Uzbekistan has been playing its part and trying to build the economy of Afghanistan. It has signed 20 MOUs and a trade deal of approximately $ 500 million. Additionally, the construction of transmission lines, the railroad and the direct air services 'Kabul – Tashkent' are some of the projects being executed through bilateral cooperation.

Uzbekistan is conscious of the fact that to prevent the spread of ISIS ideology it is important to educate youth, and towards this end, Government of Uzbekistan has taken initiative to provide assistance to Government of Afghanistan for establishing an educational center in Termez city. Both the governments also agreed to uphold four principles to build mutual trust. First, respect for sovereignty, independence, territorial integrity and national unity. Second, support the Afghan Government to begin direct negotiations with the Taliban without any preconditions. Third, provide joint assistance to promote peace, progress and socio-economic development in Afghanistan, Fourth, recognition of the importance of international and regional initiatives to ensure peace and stability in Afghanistan. It is the endeavor of the Uzbekistan government to provide practical assistance in reconstruction of Afghanistan's infrastructure, and consider it as an indispensable part, in building peace and prosperity of the country.

Uzbekistan's Approaches to Counter Extremist-Terrorist Threat

The Uzbekistan's approaches to counter violent extremism are as follows: -.

Firstly, Uzbekistan is vigorously implementing the 'Strategy of Actions' on five priority directions of development of the Republic of Uzbekistan. From 2017-2021, priority areas of the strategy are: -

(a) Re-energize system of reconstruction of state.

(b) Implementation of rule of law and judicial system.

(c) Economic development and liberalization.

(d) Creation of societal space.

(e) Security, inter-ethnic harmony and religious tolerance, and implementation of balanced, mutually beneficial and constructive foreign policy.

With the current reforms Uzbekistan is committed to implement new measures to fight terrorism and violent extremism. The President of Uzbekistan has laid down priorities for implementation in the following fields:

(a) Persuade people to return to the mainstream, especially those who are unwilling recruits by religious extremist groups.

(b) Rendering assistance for their return to mainstream.

(c) No stigmatization of those who return to the mainstream.

In addition, in 2018 the "Law on countering extremism" was proclaimed. It guides the national policy to deal with extremism, especially in detection of offenses, countering religious extremism and international cooperation in dealing with transnational terrorism. The law strictly prohibits violent extremist activities in the country and any of their manifestations.

Secondly, Uzbekistan had paid attention to strengthen cooperation within international and regional structures in developing common positions and approaches to oppose religious extremism. Today not a single country or region is immune to the threat from radicalism and terrorism. Effective measures against such phenomena can be undertaken only by international cooperation at regional and global levels. Uzbekistan supports the counter-terrorism initiatives under the aegis of the United Nations, the Organisation for Security and Co-operation in Europe (OSCE), Shanghai

Cooperation Organisation (SCO), Center for Internet Security (CIS) and other organisations that are working to counter the terrorist and extremist threat. Further, the political environment in Central Asia is working to deny space to radicals and transnational terror groups. Central Asian countries have come together to build consensus and cooperate against radicalisation and terrorism.

Thirdly, we are convinced that the use of military means in combating radicalism and terrorism is not the right way forward. As military can only tackle the consequences of the emerging challenges, and not the root cause. The main generator of radicalism, in our view, is the ideology of extremism and violence itself, which is based on ignorance and lack of tolerance. The International Research Center of Imam Bukhari, the Center for Islamic Civilization and the Islamic Academy were established in Uzbekistan and the motto of the institute is "Education against Ignorance". To increase efficiency and effectiveness of the efforts of the international community, President Sh.Mirziyoyev had initiated measures to adopt the UN General Assembly resolution on "Education and religious tolerance" along with development of the UN "International Convention on Youth Rights". The resolution on "Education and Religious Tolerance" which was adopted and supported by all UN member States in 2018 implies promotion of education, peace, human rights, tolerance and friendship. It also had recognised the importance of integration, mutual respect, human rights protection, tolerance and reciprocal understanding in maintaining international peace and security.

7

Pakistan and Cross Border Terrorism

Dr. Ajai Sahni

The expression 'cross border terrorism' has a contemporary ring to it and appears to encourage us to believe that this is a modern phenomenon. However, patterns that broadly conform to such a description, including the injection of *provocateurs* into an adversary state, the subversion of populations, fomenting and facilitating violence among disaffected sections of the population, sabotage and covert operations using irregular formations, and campaigns intended to intimidate and terrorise populations in the target state, have always played a part in warfare through human history.

Contemporary terrorism has, however, been transformed by the rapidly evolving technologies of the 20th and 21st Centuries, which have given terrorists an unprecedented mobility and lethality, even as the threat of conventional wars has progressively diminished, particularly in regions under a 'nuclear umbrella'. Terrorism has, consequently, in many cases moved significantly from the margins of inter-state conflict to its core.

No state system in the world has exploited this shift with the efficacy and to the extent to which Pakistan has harnessed this instrumentality to its perceived strategic goals. In doing this, Pakistan has arrogated to itself a role and an importance in international affairs far out of proportion to its natural strategic significance. This is a result, essentially, of its sustained and constantly adaptable engagement in cross border and global[1] terrorism.

---

1   See, for instance, "Pakistan: The Footprints of Terror," South Asia Terrorism Portal, https://www.satp.org/islamist-extremism/jan2004/pakistan-the-footprints-of-terror-america-europe.

It is, however, crucial to understand that Pakistan's cross border terrorist misadventures are rooted in its experience with the anti-Soviet 'jihad' in Afghanistan, when great power rivalry provoked the West, led by the U.S., to massively fund and arm what the Americans then described as "brave *mujahiddeen*" and "anti-Soviet warriors", through the agency of the Pakistan Army and its Inter-Services Intelligence (ISI).[2] Indeed, the emergence and sustainability of state sponsored and cross border terrorism remains inexorably linked to great power policies and strategies, both in terms of active encouragement and support, as well as in subsequent failures to act effectively, once 'rogue' operations and behaviour – that is, actions that conflict with the supporting great powers' interests – become the norm. Indeed, the common thread across theatres is that the great powers have initiated and sustained most cross-border terrorism in our age – explicitly or implicitly – and Pakistan's mischief in its neighbourhood is no exception. Further, there is a tendency, when speaking of cross border terrorism, to focus overwhelmingly on the terrorist formations that do the principal mischief on the ground. It is useful, here, to recognize explicitly that it is, in fact, Pakistan's Inter-Services Intelligence (ISI) that is the principal terrorist organisation in South Asia, and that all other major entities that are often named in the context of on-going terrorism in and from this region are essentially its agents and instrumentalities.[3] These various terrorist formations germinated, evolved and thrive under the direct protection and support of the ISI and Pakistan's military apparatus, and have long served Pakistan's purported strategic goals: 'strategic depth' and the installation of a puppet government in Afghanistan; and its campaigns to inflict relentless harm on India.

It was during the anti-Soviet campaigns in Afghanistan that Rawalpindi hardened its strategies of cross-border terrorism. Perhaps the

---

2   Afghanistan was just one of the numerous covert and violent 'cross border' interventions engineered by the U.S. through the Cold War. The U.S. has done much worse after the collapse of the Soviet Union. See, for instance, Steve Coll, *Ghost Wars: The Secret History of the CIA*, Penguin, 2015; Lindsay O'Rourke, *Covert Regime Change: America's Secret Cold War*, Cornell University Press, 2018; Stephen Kinzer, *Overthrow: America's Century of Regime Change from Hawaii to Iraq*, Times Books, 2007; Amy B. Zegart, *Spying Blind: The CIA, the FBI and the Origins of 9/11*, Princeton University Press, 2009; Joby Warrick, *Black Flags: The Rise of ISIS*, Doubleday, 2015, among others.

3   "The Core of Islamist Terror", Written evidence submitted by Dr Ajai Sahni, Institute for Conflict Management, Select Committee on Foreign Affairs Written Evidence, October 29, 2006, https://publications.parliament.uk/pa/cm200607/cmselect/cmfaff/55/55we16. htm.

most authoritative account of the strategy in Afghanistan and its further efflorescence into theatres elsewhere, is provided by a former ISI officer who was involved with the operationalisation of the strategy:

> Death by a thousand cuts – this is the time-honoured tactic of the guerrilla army against a large conventional force... Ambushes, assassinations, attacks on supply convoys, bridges, pipelines, and airfields, with the avoidance of set piece battles; these are history's proven techniques for the guerrilla... eventually, the tactics of a thousand cut would produce *such a haemorrhaging of men and money that the burden would be unbearable.*[4]

Somewhat obliquely, late General Zia ul Haq, Pakistan's then dictator, had told the then Chief of the ISI, Lt. Gen. Akhtar Abdul Rehman Khan in 1979, "The water in Afghanistan must boil at the right temperature."[5] This, again, is a core element of the 'war of a thousand cuts': the calibration of cross border violence to appropriate levels, reflecting evolving circumstances in a particular theatre. Thus, a dramatic decline in violence –does not reflect any abandonment or even dilution of the basic objective or strategy. Rather, they reflect transient tactical and operational adaptations to an adverse situation (from Rawalpindi's perspective). The most dramatic case in point was the scenario that developed in the AF-Pak theatre in the immediate aftermath of 9/11, when the then U.S. Assistant Secretary of State, Richard Armitage told Pakistan's then Dictator, President General Pervez Musharraf, that Pakistan would be "bombed back into the stone age".[6] Pakistan had focused its attention on facilitating the Taliban's relocation to Pakistani soil, but there was a dramatic suspension of operations from Pakistan into Afghanistan for some months, till the gaps in the U.S. strategy began to show, and Rawalpindi once again restored Taliban operations into Afghanistan under the direction of the newly established Quetta Shura.

Pakistan's involvement in Afghanistan and subsequently in Jammu & Kashmir has long been an open secret, explicitly acknowledged by leaders, but opportunistically denied in international forums, where Islamabad

---

4   Mohammad Yousaf & Mark Adkin, *The Bear Trap: Afghanistan's Untold Story*, Jang Publishers, 1992, pp. 1 & 3, emphasis added.

5   Ibid. p. 20.

6   Suzanne Goldenberg, "Bush threatened to bomb Pakistan, says Musharraf", *The Guardian*, September 22, 2006, https://www.theguardian.com/world/2006/sep/22/pakistan.usa.

seeks to project itself as a 'victim of terrorism'. It is useful to recall, that successive regimes in the U.S. have acknowledged Pakistan's role in cross border terrorism and, as far back as in the 1990s, Pakistan was at the cusp of being declared a state sponsor of terrorism by Washington on at least two occasions, in 1992 and 1998.[7] In 2017, U.S. President Donald Trump had declared:

"We can no longer be silent about Pakistan's safe havens for terrorist organisations, the Taliban, and other groups that pose a threat to the region and beyond. Pakistan has much to gain from partnering with our effort in Afghanistan. It has much to lose by continuing to harbor criminals and terrorists."[8]

In 2011, the then U.S. Secretary of State Hillary Clinton warned Pakistan, "you can't keep snakes in your backyard and expect them only to bite your neighbours."[9]Even Pakistani establishment figures, on several occasions, have admitted to supporting these terrorist formations and using them for cross border terrorism. Most recently, Pakistan's Prime Minister Imran Khan conceded

"...But I can tell you one thing, you see, I again go back. The Pakistani Army, ISI, trained al-Qaida and all these troops to fight in Afghanistan. There were always links between — there had to be links, because they trained them..."[10]

Earlier, General Pervez Musharraf had admitted to the country's role in cross border terrorism in Jammu & Kashmir, observing,

"In 1990s the freedom struggle began in Kashmir... At that time Lashkar-e-Taiba (LeT) and 11 or 12 other organisations were formed. We supported them and trained them as they were fighting in Kashmir

---

7   Jeffrey Goldberg and Marc Ambinder, "The Ally from Hell", *The Atlantic*, December 2011.

8   Donald Trump's speech on South Asia policy. Remarks by President Trump on the Strategy in Afghanistan and South Asia, August 21, 2017 https://www.satp.org/document/paper-acts-and-oridinances/donald-trump-s-speech-on-south-asia-policy

9   Rezaul H. Laskar, "Pak can't keep snakes in backyard: US", *Hindustan Times*, October 22, 2011.

10 A Conversation With Prime Minister Imran Khan of Pakistan, *Council on Foreign Relations*, September 23, 2019, https://www.cfr.org/event/conversation-prime-minister-imran-khan-pakistan-0

at the cost of their lives…The Kashmiri freedom fighters including Hafiz Saeed and Lakhvi were our heroes at that time. Later on the religious militancy turned into terrorism."[11]

Astonishingly, despite repeated acceptance, both by the Pakistani and the world leadership, of Pakistan's role in creating and sustaining cross border and global terrorism, pockets of Western support continue to propagate the notion of an increasingly incredible 'credible deniability'.

Afghanistan

While the devastation, which Pakistan has wrought in Afghanistan, is substantially a consequence of enabling factors injected by the U.S. and the West, it is useful to recognise that Rawalpindi's cross border meddling in Afghanistan predates the U.S. intervention, to the time when the then Afghanistan President Mohammad Daoud had launched a campaign against Afghan Islamists, who then sought safe haven in Pakistan. Many among these Islamists had later become leaders of the anti-Soviet resistance, with Gulbuddin Hekmatyar the most prominent among them. Hekmatyar had become a trusted friend and ally of the ISI. Later, when U.S. coalition resources began to flow into the conflict, it was Hekmatyar who had received the lion's share of the assistance distributed through the ISI.[12]

The Soviet intrusion into Afghanistan and immediate call for resistance by the U.S. vastly augmented Pakistan's capacities for destabilisation in Afghanistan. The U.S. aided and abetted Pakistan's ISI to launch cross border attacks into Afghanistan, targeting the Soviet Forces. Islamabad helped Hekmatyar and other proxies to create terror in Afghanistan, eventually engineering the withdrawal of Soviet Forces in 1989. Despite his success against the Soviets, Hekmatyar had failed to capture Kabul, and consequently failed to secure Pakistan's influence over Afghanistan. Islamabad had shifted its support to a new force, the Taliban, a movement of religious students (Talibs), who rapidly established dominance in the

---

11 "Pakistan supported, trained terror groups to carry out militancy in Kashmir: Pervez Musharraf," *Economic Times*, July 12, 2018, https://economictimes.indiatimes.com/news/defence/pakistan-supported-trained-terror-groups-to-carry-out-militancy-in-kashmir-pervez-musharraf/articleshow/49563327.cms

12 Najib Lafraie, "Post-Soviet Pakistani Interference in Afghanistan: How and Why", *Middle East Institute*, April 18, 2012, https://www.mei.edu/publications/post-soviet-pakistani-interference-afghanistan-how-and-why

south of the country, bordering Pakistan. The Taliban went on to take over most of Afghanistan by the late 1990s,[13] with a heroic resistance eventually limited to the country's Northeast, by the Tajik dominated Northern Alliance led by the legendary Ahmad Shah Massoud. He was assassinated by al Qaeda on September 2, 2001, two days before the 9/11 attacks in the U.S.. It is useful to recall Massoud's words here:

> "The Taliban are not a force to be considered invincible. They are distanced from the people now. They are weaker than in the past. There is only the assistance given by Pakistan, Osama bin Laden and other extremist groups that keep the Taliban on their feet. With a halt to that assistance, it is extremely difficult to survive. We hope that the future policy of the U.S. will exert pressure on Pakistan and also help Afghanistan achieve peace. That would be much more effective than giving [us] weapons or ammunition."[14]

Bin Laden is dead, but Pakistan's assistance remains decisive in the Taliban's survival and progressive strengthening even today, and the perpetually elusive 'pressure on Pakistan' remains the key to any possible and lasting resolution of the 'Afghan problem'. 9/11 returned Afghanistan to the core of U.S. foreign policy concerns, and Washington re-entered the conflict in that country after a hiatus of over a decade. In the intervening years since, the U.S. has suffered 2,441 military fatalities,[15] and this has sufficed to make a rapid withdrawal from the theatre a sufficiently urgent policy priority to force a direct negotiation with the Taliban, sidelining the elected government at Kabul. These negotiations were to culminate in a summit at Camp David in September 2019, but the move was scuttled in the wake of a suicide attack in Kabul that had killed 12 persons, including an American soldier, in what the Americans described as an attempt to secure "false leverage" in the negotiations.[16] The U.S. has already

---

13 Sanchita Bhattacharya, "Afghanistan: HIG: Volatile Player, *South Asia Intelligence Review*, Volume 10, No. 19, November 14, 2011https://www.satp.org/satporgtp/sair/Archives/sair10/10_19.htm

14 "Massoud's Last Words," *Newsweek*, September 19, 2001, https://www.newsweek.com/massouds-last-words-151823.

15 *icasualties.org*, "Fatalities by Year and Country: Afghanistan," http://icasualties.org, accessed on December 25 2019.

16 John Bowden and Morgan Chalfant, Trump Cancels Secret Meeting with Taliban, Afghan President, after attack, *The Hill*, September 7, 2019, https://thehill.com/homenews/administration/460396-trump-cancels-secret-meeting-with-taliban-

spent USD 975 billion in the war since 2001 (including projections for 2019).[17] More significantly, the impact on Afghanistan has been devastating, with well over an estimated 111,000 deaths,[18] millions disabled, millions of others displaced, and no foreseeable prospects of any return to an acceptable level of peace and normalcy. Afghanistan was second from the very bottom of the Global Peace Index, 2018, at the 162nd position out of 163 countries, just above Syria.[19]

India

The expulsion of Soviet forces from Afghanistan fed the myth of an 'Islamist victory' over one of the world's superpowers, and the Pakistan military establishment had gained tremendous confidence from the experience, marginalizing the significance of U.S. and global support, as well as of the Afghan resistance, and feeding the illusion that the Pakistan Army was the principal architect of this victory. With a significant proportion of its proxies freed from the Afghan campaigns, Pakistan had turned its attention, and its surplus of irregulars, to its enduring obsession with Kashmir and the 'unfinished agenda' of Partition, as well as with avenging the country's own vivisection in 1971.

However, it is important to emphasize that Pakistan's terrorism across the Indian border did not commence at this stage. Pakistan had already been playing a pivotal role in the Khalistan insurgency in Punjab, providing safe haven, weaponry and resources to the militants and facilitating their operations across the border. Border crossings remained a continuous and daily occurrence along the 533 kilometer long international border Punjab shared with Pakistan, and could never really be effectively checked, despite 122 kilometer of fencing that had been erected by August 1989.[20]

---

leaders-afghan-president.

17 Kimberly Amadeo, "Afghanistan War Cost, Timeline, and Economic Impact, *The Balance*, updated June 15, 2019, https://www.thebalance.com/cost-of-afghanistan-war-timeline-economic-impact-4122493.

18 Neta C. Crawford, Update on the Human Costs of War for Afghanistan and Pakistan, 2001 to mid-2016, Watson Institute, Brown University, https://watson.brown.edu/costsofwar/files/cow/imce/papers/2016/War%20in%20Afghanistan%20and%20Pakistan%20UPDATE_FINAL_corrected%20date.pdf.

19 *Global Peace Index 2018*, Institute for Economics and Peace, http://visionofhumanity.org/app/uploads/2018/06/Global-Peace-Index-2018-2.pdf, p. 9.

20 KPS Gill, "Endgame In Punjab: 1988-1993", *Faultlines: Writings on Conflict & Resolution*, Volume- 1, May-1999, https://satp.org/faultline-chapter-details/volume-1/

Partial data compiled by the *Institute for Conflict Management* (ICM), has records at least 21,677 terrorism linked fatalities in the Punjab since 1988.[21] Eventually, when the Khalistan had come under near-terminal pressure in the early 1990s, the ISI had authored its 'K2' programme - a plot to bring together Khalistani and Kashmiri terrorists. The project was an abject failure, but the ISI has continued its efforts.[22]

It would also be a mistake to date the commencement of cross border terrorism in Jammu & Kashmir to the withdrawal of the Soviet Forces from Afghanistan. Indeed, Pakistan's cross border terrorism had commenced at the very moment of Independence, when tribal irregulars were pushed into the then Princely State. After accession to India, the Indian Army was able to push the Pakistani forces back to what is now the Line of Control, leaving 'Azad Kashmir' and Gilgit Baltistan under Pakistan's control. Pakistan's efforts at destabilisation and cross border terrorism thereafter were sustained, if low grade.[23] The conflict that escalated to unprecedented proportions after the Rubaiya Sayeed abduction in late 1989 was, in fact, a culmination of a 'five-decade old secret war'.

Since 1988, according to the official data, at least 45,298 fatalities (14,125 civilians, 5,236 Security Force (SF) personnel, and 25,715 militants) have been recorded in J&K as a result of Pakistan backed terrorism (data till December 31, 2018).[24] Outside J&K, Pakistan backed Islamist terrorism has resulted in a further 1,328 fatalities (999 civilians, 56 SF personnel, 157 militants and 116 Not Specified) between March 6, 2000 and September 25, 2019.[25] Pakistan has sent thousands of terrorists trained in the *jihad* factories operating on its soil into India. According to official data, between

---

endgame-in-punjab-1988-93

21 Annual Fatalities in terrorist related violence 1981-2018, SATP, http://old.satp.org/satporgtp/countries/india/states/punjab/data_sheets/annual_casualties.htm

22 KPS Gill, "ISI has persisted with its 'K2' plan to bring together Khalistani and Kashmiri terrorists", November 5, 2011, *India Today*, https://www.indiatoday.in/magazine/cover-story/story/20111114-k-p s gill-on-isi-khalistan-militants-749542-2011-11-05

23 For a detailed examination of Pakistan's unrelenting efforts over the decades, see Praveen Swami, *India, Pakistan and the Secret Jihad*, Routledge, 2013.

24 MHA Data on Fatalities in Jammu and Kashmir: 1990-2018, https://satp.org/official-data/jammukashmir/fatalities-jammu-kashmir-mha-data

25 Datasheet - ISLAMIST/OTHER CONFLICTS, SATP, https://satp.org/datasheet-terrorist-attack/fatalities/india islamistotherconflicts

1997 and 2001 alone, at least 10,221 militant infiltrations were detected[26] and 10,354 estimated infiltrations took place between 2001 and 2016. [27] In order to facilitate terrorist infiltration, Pakistan keeps the border volatile. Though no comprehensive data is available on border firing prior to the 2003 Cease Fire Agreement (CFA), official data for the period between 2004 and 2019 has indicated at least 6,537 CFA violations by Pakistan (data till June 30, 2019). [28]

Pakistan has also used radical and/or separatist elements within India's frontiers to sustain its proxy war. In case of J&K, the role played by the separatist groups in helping Pakistan sustain its proxy war has been well established. A summary of case registered by National Investigation Agency (NIA) on May 30, 2017, thus reads,

> "Credible information has been received by the Central Government that Hafiz Muhammad Saeed, Amir of Jammat-ud-Dawah and the secessionist and separatist leaders, including the members of the Hurriyat Conference, have been acting in connivance with active militants of proscribed terrorist organisations Hizb-ul-Mujahideen (HM), Dukhtarane Millat, Lashkar-e-Toiba (LeT) and other terrorist organisations for raising, receiving and collecting funds domestically and abroad through various illegal channels, including hawala, for funding separatist and terrorist activities in Jammu and Kashmir, through the funds so collected and as such have entered into a larger criminal conspiracy for causing disruption in the Kashmir valley by way of pelting stones on the security forces, systematically burning schools, damage to public property and waging war against India."[29]

The case of the Indian Mujahideen (IM), which has survived due to Pakistan's support, is similar. Mr. Stephen Tankel has observed,

> "...external support was a force multiplier for Indian militancy rather

---

26   Infiltration detected in Jammu and Kashmir from January 1997 to May, 2002, SATP, https://satp.org/officialdata/jammukashmir/infiltration.aspx

27   Estimated Infiltration in J&K, SATP, https://satp.org/officialdata/jammukashmir/estimated-infiltration-in-jk.aspx

28 Cease-fire Agreement (CFA) Violations by Pakistan in Jammu and Kashmir: 2004-2019, SATP, https://satp.org/official-data/jammukashmir/cfa-violations

29 Funding to separatist organisation in J&K, Case Number RC-10/2017/NIA/DLI, https://www.nia.gov.in/case-detail.htm?169

than a key driver of it. Although the IM receives support from LeT, it should not be viewed as an affiliate within the same command-and-control hierarchy. This distinguishes the IM from some of the other LeT cells or operatives active in India…"[30]

As in the case of Afghanistan, Pakistan's role in cross border terrorism in India has been well documented and acknowledged. An unnamed former Indian intelligence official observes, "We have known about its (S Wing's) existence for several years. It took shape probably in the '80s, and from then on it has grown in size and strength." Further, the entire operation of Kashmir militancy, over the preceding 20 years, had been handled by the ISI's 'S Wing'.[31] On July 9, 2012, the then acting Director General of Police (DGP), J&K, K. Rajendra, noted, "No terrorist activity can take place in our country without the support of the actors from across the border… There are state actors headed by the ISI."[32]

A Paradigm of Response

The problem in Afghanistan, as in Kashmir, is Pakistan, and an enduring solution to these conflicts can only be found, if this reality becomes the critical pivot of global and regional responses. Despite increasing global recognition of Pakistan's role in cross-border and global terrorism, the world community has refused to act effectively against Pakistan. Despite some symbolic efforts to pressure Rawalpindi and Islamabad, they had continued to cede Pakistan a central position in efforts to secure an impossible 'negotiated settlement' with the Taliban, which could purportedly bring peace and civilized governance in Afghanistan.

India, similarly, has floundered in a reactive, contradictory and counter-productive paradigm of response. For decades, Delhi had remained committed to unsubstantiated dogmas, that a 'strong and stable Pakistan is in India's interests' and that 'one cannot choose one's neighbours'. India

30 Stephen Tankel, "Jihadist Violence: The Indian Threat", Woodrow Wilson International Center, https://www.wilsoncenter.org/sites/default/files/stephentankelreportIndianmilitancyfinalversion_0.pdf

31 "Chicago trial puts focus on shadowy S Wing of ISI", *The Times of India*, May 28, 2011, https://timesofindia.indiatimes.com/india/Chicago-trial-puts-focus-on-shadowy-S-Wing-of-ISI/articleshow/8612217.cms,

32 Sanchita Bhattacharya, "ISI: Twisted Shadows, *South Asia Intelligence Review*, Volume 11, No. 16, October 22, 2012, https://www.satp.org/satporgtp/sair/Archives/sair11/11_16.htm#assessment1

is, perhaps, unique among Nations to argue that a strong and stable enemy is in its interests. As for choosing neighbors, the evidence of history is that neighbours and neighbourhood change constantly. A single proximate example should suffice in evidence; the Eastern wing of Pakistan had become Bangladesh in 1971, while Pakistan was able to salvage some influence in Bangladesh till the early 2000s, thereafter, Bangladesh has been more than cooperative in India's efforts to contain insurgency and terrorism. Especially, since the Sheikh Hasina regime was installed in 2009. At least one of India's neighbours has been changed.

War, 'limited war', tit-for-tat support to separatist and terrorist formations in Pakistan, and retaliatory action across the border has all been furiously, albeit erratically, debated. As, indeed, have 'peace processes' and 'negotiated settlements', usually with extremely limited and fitful outcome. What has largely been missed in all this is that there has been wide variety of instrumentalities that can be directed against Pakistan, which obviate the use of military means or retaliatory support to militancy and terrorism. This indeed, leaves purported 'peace processes' undisturbed as 'other means are deployed to weaken the adversary's position. What is required for such an approach to be conceived and implemented, however, is the state's commitment to a strategy over the long term, and not the "policy pendulum"[33], that has afflicted India's counter-terrorism and Pakistan policies over the decades, and that continues to create spaces for mischief even today.[34] As has been noted elsewhere,

> "A fitting reply can only be formulated within the context of a protracted conflict paradigm. This requires all institutions in Pakistan to be targeted in an enduring campaign that harnesses every aspect of state power in India over an extended period of time, exploiting Pakistan's vulnerabilities and eroding its limited strengths. This requires a doctrine, a strategy, the acquisition of capacities and capabilities, and the continuous deployment of tactical interventions. None of this appears to be within the ken of those who run this

---

33 Ajai Sahni, "Another Swing of the Pendulum," *South Asia Intelligence Review*, Vol. 2.No. 16, November 3, 2003, https://www.satp.org/publication/ajaisahni/WarWithinBorderDetails.aspx?Id=252.

34 Ajai Sahni, "Kartarpur Corridor: Twisted Calculus," Second Sight, Vol. 1, No. 3, November 29, 2018, https://www.satp.org/publication/ajaisahni/WarWithinBorderDetails.aspx?Id=334; "Kartarpur: Reckless throw of the dice," *Hindustan Times*, December 14, 2018, https://www.hindustantimes.com/analysis/kartarpur-reckless-throw-of-the-dice/story-3VuUnaGwyZSkWofG9LbHGJ.html.

country — or who have run this country over decades in the past."[35]

It is imperative, consequently, that India's past approach to Pakistan's cross border terrorism, deeply flawed and riddled with inconsistencies, be completely reviewed, and an alternative policy framework be defined to inform the perspectives and decisions of all sections of government.[36] Within this context, it is necessary to emphasise the incoherence of widely prevailing and enduring perspectives within the higher policy making echelons that have, first, long operated on the faith that 'destabilizing' Pakistan would have an adverse impact on India. And, further, by a curious inversion of responsibility, argued that India must 'work' towards creating a strong, stable and 'democratic' Pakistan (a peculiar ambition for a polity that is unable to engineer a strong and stable democracy even within its own territories). Within this broad framework, a dominant presumption seems to be that the conversion of the Line of Control (LoC) into an international border (IB) is the 'only possible solution' to the Kashmir imbroglio.

At the core of a coherent strategy of response to Pakistan's cross border terrorism is the idea that the conflict in Kashmir, while it must continue to be fought with great urgency at a tactical level, must also be seen within a far more extended time perspective than is currently the case. Within such a time perspective, it must be recognized that Pakistan's existence is itself in question, hence, its claims on Kashmir, does not need to be taken as a permanent thing, 'given' in the geo-strategic equation; nor in any particular formulation – including the conversion of the LoC into the IB (any necessary part of an eventual resolution). Significantly, the very nature of the Pakistani state – specifically, the marriage of Islamist and military institutions – implies that any transitional solution, such as the transformation of the LoC into the IB, cannot permanently alter the character of relations between the two countries. Pakistan will not – and cannot – abandon its long-term agenda towards India unless it undergoes a radical ideological and political transformation. Such a transformation is

---

35 Aishwarya Kumar, "Pakistan Has 'All-weather' Supporters, Diplomatic Isolation Won't Help Much: Counter-terrorism Expert Ajai Sahni", News 18, March 7, 2019, https.// www.news18.com/news/india/pakistan-has-all-weather-supporters-diplomatic-isolation-wont-help-much-counter-terrorism-expert-ajai-sahni-2058925.html

36 This section, and the components of the strategic response herein, rely principally on a note submitted by K.P.S. Gill and this writer to the then Minister of Home Affairs in 2002.

not within the realm of foreseeable possibilities, nor do the instrumentalities to secure any such transformation exist in Pakistan.

India's 'end state' objectives with regard to Pakistan must, consequently, incorporate the possibility of a 'regime change' that transforms – or destroys – the existing state structure in Pakistan. Such a regime change would ideally replace the combined power of the Islamist jehadi-feudal-militarist, that currently rules the country, with a constitutional, democratic, non-discriminatory, secular 'open society', whose ideological ends are not in fundamental opposition to those held by the Indian state. Such an end state is unlikely, and India lacks the leverage and mechanisms to bring about such change.

Consequently, in the absence of such an ideal outcome, the gradual erosion and dismantling of the Pakistani state should be recognized as a clear objective of India's state policy. This must be pursued relentlessly through every means available within a protracted war framework – including, primarily, a range of competitive strategies that embrace economic measures, diplomacy, subversion, propaganda, an escalated arms race and military attrition.

The overall 'competitive strategy' that will have to be designed and executed to achieve these ends will require inputs from, and coordination between, a number of departments and ministries, and will have to be coherently implemented over an extended period of time. It would, consequently, be desirable to set up a separate 'cell' or 'mission' to oversee the definition and realization of this strategy. To the extent that a multiplicity of agencies and ministries would be involved, such a cell would be most effective, if it is suitably empowered and located within the existing structures of the government, under the charge of a high-profile advisor on internal security. The existence and operation of this cell must be covert and deeply concealed from public and international view.

Crucially, this competitive strategy must be recognized as principally a strategy of non-military attrition and not a 'tit-for-tat' campaign of terrorism on Pakistani soil. Such latter campaigns have invariably afflicted sponsoring nations (including India, in the case of Tamil terrorism in Sri Lanka) with a 'blowback'. The idea is to bleed Pakistan with a thousand cuts – social, economic and political. Every instrumentality to secure this end is available in Pakistan itself.

Within the context of such a protracted war strategy, and the implied adoption of a coherent and consistent strategy over an extended period of time, it would be noticed that Kashmir would no longer remain the 'core issue'. The 'core issue' would be Pakistan itself, and a permanent question mark can be put against its very existence. If such an end state informs India's policy perspectives, it will be seen that Kashmir is nothing more than a 'holding operation' from the Indian point of view. Eventually, Pakistan can be sufficiently weakened and undermined to a point where its geo-political ambitions become unsustainable, if, indeed, the country cannot entirely be dismantled. Indian policies should not only acknowledge such a possibility but should work actively and vigorously towards its realization. This is the perspective that must consistently underpin the entire complex of India's policies on Pakistan-backed terrorism and towards Pakistan.

One of the central objectives of India's enduring strategy against Pakistan must be to bring Pakistan and its people to international contempt, as well as contempt in their own eyes. It is in the collapse of their own exaggerated self-perception that the necessary collapse of their will to power and warfare can be secured. Such a transformation can be advanced in power by a campaign to convince the international community and Western policy makers that a de-nuclearized and de-militarized Pakistan is not only in the interests of world peace but is essential if terrorism is to be defeated. While such an end may appear a remote and unrealistic possibility in the immediate future, Pakistan's own folly and a coherent campaign by India could improve the probabilities of bringing such an objective on the world agenda in the medium term. Even if this does not happen, putting such an idea at the center of the international discourse would exert extraordinary and unprecedented pressure on the leadership in Pakistan.

The specific policies, programmes and instruments of India's protracted war strategy against Pakistan are a matter of evolving detail; would overwhelmingly rely on covert action and cannot be addressed here. There is, nevertheless, a sufficient literature on protracted war to aid the crystallization of these elements, if and when the political will and understanding to accept such a national strategy consolidates. The principal obstacle to this is that "Continuous and irreconcilable conflict requires an organisational capacity comparable to democratic states institute only in times of war and dire crisis."[37] While India's leadership has often spoken of Pakistan's cross border terrorism as a 'proxy war', national responses have never demonstrated the urgency or scale of a reaction, to acts of warfare.

It is not Pakistan's strength or perversity alone that fuels cross border terrorism, but the infirmity of our own policies, the ignorance and opportunism of our leaderships, the inability to maintain strategic focus and aim, over an extended framework of time, and the institutional incoherence, that prevents a coordinated response across all constituents of government and national power. These are the elements that underpin enduring national vulnerabilities and create not just opportunities, but worse, positive incentive systems for the enemy's mischief.

---

37   Robert Strausz-Hupe, Willaim R. Kinlner, James E. Dougherty & Alvin J. Cottrell, *Protracted Conflict*, New York: Harper Colophon, 1963, p. 120.

8

Evolving Challenges and Radicalisation in IOR Littoral Countries

Brig Gen Zakariyya Mansoor

The Indian Ocean is the third largest water body between Africa and Asia Oceania continent that holds diverse geographic and demographic construct in the world. It spans approximately 6000 miles from East to West and covers 13 percent of the earth's surface and over 20 percent of its water body. This body of water is home to a population of over two billion, living in 37 littoral countries. The Indian Ocean also holds crucial energy resources that feed a booming global industry. This busy International Shipping Lanes (ISLs) holds a stake of 80 per cent of world's global maritime trade and 60 percent of energy trade. Stability and peace in the IOR littoral are imperative to sustain international trade and uninterrupted energy supply across the globe.

The safety of energy and trade routes in the Indian Ocean is dependent on the security of choke points and ISLs. The freedom of navigation enjoyed by vessels passing through the choke points of the Indian Ocean remains the fulcrum, which has kept the maritime trade flowing through the ocean. These choke points include the Malacca Straits, Sunda Strait, Lombok Strait, Strait of Hormuz, Gulf of Aden (Bab-el Mandeb/Suez Canal), Mozambique Channel and the Cape of Good Hope. Approximately, 40 percent of the total oil tankers pass through the Strait of Hormuz.

Due to trade and energy, IOR has also become one of the most volatile water bodies in the world. In recent years, IOR has experienced spread of terrorism in littoral states along with maritime piracy, an increase in drug trafficking, gun running, maritime terrorism and Illegal Unregulated and Unreported (IUU) fishing. Other non-traditional threats such as natural disasters have also made region prone to instability and mass relocation of population.

Radicalisation: A Threat in the Indian Ocean Region

Among all the threats stated above, the IOR is home to 42 percent of conflicts in the world. The conflicts are connected to resource control, radicalisation and transnational terrorism. In the absence of regional security architecture, the state and non-state actors across the IOR are pushing their agenda and ideologies in pursuance of their political objectives. The Middle East, North Africa, Afghanistan, and Pakistan (MENAP) remain the most affected region as well as the cradle of transnational terrorism. Groups such as Al-Shabab in Somalia and Boko Haram in Nigeria are creating havoc and spreading Islamist ideologies in Africa.

In the Arab Sea belt, Al-Qaeda and Islamic State are competing with each other to spread their ideologies. The ISIS and Al Qaeda affiliates such as Hurras al-Din and Hayath Tahrir al-Sham are attracting recruits from IOR and even beyond to fight, to establish the Islamic Caliphate. In the recent past, two major terror attacks were carried out in South Asia; Mumbai 26/11, where 174 people were killed and Easter Attack in Sri Lanka in 2019, where more than 250 people were killed.

The Easter Sunday attack in Sri Lanka on April 21, 2019 was also a wake-up call on utilisation and motivation of sleeper cells to carry out devastating suicide attacks by self-radicalized members of a family. It was one of the worst attacks since the days of LTTE, the string of attacks took 259 lives. The local Islamist group, the National Thowheeth Jama'ath, a group known to be affiliated with IS, carried out these attacks. The founder of the group, Zahran Hashim was a known figure and a preacher with extremist ideologies. Despite the fact that he was accused of spreading violent ideologies, somehow police did not make any efforts to prevent him from carrying out violent attacks.

Some of the most populous states in the Indian Ocean Region, Bangladesh and Indonesia, are also prone to radicalisation by the ideologies of IS and Al Qaeda. IS related groups such as the Jamatul Mujahideen Bangladesh (JMB), Bangladesh Jamaat-e-Islami and other small radical groups have carried out attacks in Bangladesh. The recruitment and radicalisation among the persecuted Rohingyas have also increased, and Al Qaeda and IS ideologies have infiltrated the Rohingya armed groups. Indonesia, is the most populous state in terms of the Islamic faith, has also been swarmed by targeted radicalisation. From the devastating Bali bombing in 2002 by Jemaah Islamiyah, to the current attacks by Jamaah Ansharut Daulah, Indonesia also faces challenges in countering the radicalisation of its youth.

The successful recruitment of youth into these groups, inspired by the extremist ideologies is an indicator of the challenge; states face to counter the spread of Islamists ideology and radicalisation. It has been estimated that well over 40,000 foreign fighters were involved during the hype of IS in Syria and Iraq. Among these, most of the fighters were from Arab countries and also countries in the Indian sub-continent.

Sub-Regional Context

South Asia is a region that is diverse in terms of demography, religion, culture and political ideologies. South Asia has about 651 million Muslims which is one third of South Asia's population. 62 percent of the world's Muslims live in Asia with Indonesia, Pakistan, India and Bangladesh being the four largest Muslim nations in the world. South Asia is among the regions in the world with highest annual number of fatalities caused by terrorist violence. Lately, the issue of grave concern has been the rise of radicalisation. There are several reasons which accounts for this rise. One of them is anti-American sentiment. The unconditional support from the U.S. to Israel and their backing of oppressive regimes, especially in the Middle East attributed to this Anti-American sentiment.

However, there are more local reasons for radicalisation of Muslims in Asia. Regional wars, unresolved conflicts and a series of global events are the reasons that have contributed to the spread of radicalisation. The lack of ideological alternatives and absence of powerful narrative has also led to the rise of radicalisation. Uneven development pattern and not addressing the grievances of the population, is also contributing to the spread of radical ideology The mosques and madrassas across the region have been used as primary platforms for ideological motivation and recruitment by terrorist groups. There is no shortcut to eliminating the threat of radicalisation in the region without formulating a comprehensive approach to deal with the issue.

The Maldives Context

Maldives has been an Islamic country since the 12th century and Maldivian society was largely moderate for much of history since then. As madrassah education in the region had become accessible during the 80s that provided the students free education with meals and clothing, it had given an opportunity for many Maldivian citizens to send their children to undertake Islamic education in those countries. The return of these students after completing their studies with more extreme and conservative ideologies was one of the main cause of import of extremism into the Maldivian society.

It is a country that consists of 100 percent Sunni Muslim population of around 350,000, scattered over two hundred inhabited islands. These physical factors cause problems such as unequal development between rural and urban areas, isolation and lack of access to infrastructure; areas with high population density and other areas where populations are too small to be economically viable. Despite this, Maldivians have enjoyed the highest GDP per capita in the South Asian region. However, the distribution of wealth amongst the populace is disproportionate; further, overcrowding in population centres such as the greater Male' area and lack of employment opportunities in other islands create division among the people.

Spread of Extremism in Maldives

Religious matters were controlled by the state under the '1994 Protection of Religious Unity Act' and the formation of the 'Islamic Council' for regulating religious affairs in the country. There were number of clashes between extremist clerics and the government which resulted in the banishment of these clerics to other islands. This measure had turned catastrophic, as these clerics had begun to convert many people from the host island, to a more extremist version of Islam.

The 2004 tsunami was an opportunity exploited by regional terrorist networks to get access into the devastated islands of the Maldives. Lashkar-e-Taiba (LeT)'s charitable wing invested thousands of dollars into the tsunami hit islands in order to spread their ideologies to the people of these islands. Their charitable contributions included inviting the youth to various regional madrassahs, where they were recruited into more dangerous radical organisations. Maldivian society has harboured a number of Islamist organisations, some of whom had propagated an ultra-conservative strain of Islam. Many of the scholars and members are known to have been educated abroad. In recent years these organisations have started campaigns to raise Islamic awareness. Though there are no organised jihadi groups operating within Maldives or any group with Maldivian roots operating outside the Maldives. However, the country has proven to be disproportionately affected by recruitment drive by jihadi groups. Al Qaeda and the Islamic State have attracted and continue to successfully recruit youth from the Maldives.

Radicalisation: The Maldivian Experience

The Radicalisation Process

For the purposes of this document, radicalisation has been defined as the "process of adopting an extremist belief system including the willingness to use, support, or facilitate violence, as a method to achieve an ideological goal". As a process, radicalisation can be divided into four phases, namely, pre-radicalisation, identification, indoctrination and action. Mobilization to action based on radicalism is classified as terrorism.

Radicalisation in Maldives

The process adopted by transnational groups, is targeted radicalisation as the prevalent mode. It has also been noted that there are some self-radicalised individuals as well.

Targeted radicalisation in the Maldives is done in many ways, with mixed results. Some of those involved in these activities have been identified as trained returnees, (from the conflicts zones). Targets with inductive emotional states are identified by the ideologues. They are then targeted, taking into consideration, various socio-economic and personal factors. Notably, Maldives is a country where the capital and some other islands can be listed amongst the most densely populated areas in the world. This population density has led to issues such as high crime rates, high divorce rates, family problems and psychiatric issues. In addition, there is high unemployment rate in Maldives, and youth is unwilling to work in construction, hygiene and public health sectors. The terror organisations sell a dream of a great future, if they follow them. There have been cases where targets in weakened emotional states were identified, approached and coerced into one-on-one sessions. These sessions were used to provide spiritual education and ideological training.

Targets have included people who had relationship issues, drug users and having a criminal background, or were part of criminal gangs. These individuals were then apparently promised salvation, with joining the fight as the only option, for repentance for their particular crimes. Others were promised a better spiritual or worldly life in a caliphate with material gains.

There have also been reports of local religious NGOs conducting classes and forming secret radicalisation and recruitment networks. Individual recruiters have also been known to form closed groups, such as fishing crews or social groups. These individuals are then introduced to social media tools such as *Viber* groups and *Telegram* channels that provide them with more information on the subject covertly. In addition, schools are becoming a platform for recruitment by radical organisations. The role of teachers in recruitment was highlighted by the recent arrest of a known teacher suspected of conducting such activities for the Islamic State group.

It has been noted that the most recent subjects for targeted radicalisation have been skilled personnel, such as pilots, and ex-members of the security forces. Some of the radicalised criminal elements who have been radicalised are known to have undergone the process in prison as well. It has been known that some prisoners with extremist ideologies were given positions within the prison as Imams. This was done as they were good at recitation of Quran, than most of the other prisoners. This allowed these individuals to preach within the community and introduce their ideology to the prisoners. This made these prisoners believe that their acts of crime will be cleansed, and they will be pardoned by God Almighty.

In the case of self-radicalised individuals, sources have indicated that they are radicalised after coming across the propaganda on the internet. These individuals then find forums or social media contacts that eventually lead them to the recruiters. They are then approached through the private messaging app. Another aspect is the contact made by Maldivian foreign fighters to their family members and friends over social media. This is a phenomenon that is being repeated around the world, with IS in particularly adopting a very strong and effective social media presence. It is also noteworthy that most Maldivians who have left to fight in Syria are in their early 20s to mid-30s. This is one of their target audiences for the social media campaign.

The Maldives has faced several problems in the social, political and economic domains. It also has a population that is in touch with the world (due to high internet and communications penetration) and is educated. This has led to high expectations and standard of living when it comes to personal lives. In addition, social and economic expectations were not met for various reasons, resulting in despair. These youths find solace in religious discourse and they seek their identity through religion. Portrayal of Islam as radical religion by the West is also seen as an attempt by the youths to malign their faith and religion. It creates insecurity and youth find refuge in the radical hard-line form of Islam. Societal rejection, humiliation or victimisation, actual or perceived, leads to the perception of rejection or negations; as a result it increases ontological insecurity.

Countering the Challenges

Among the large populations in the littorals of the IOR, a substantial number have lived in poverty. The competition for resources, such as energy, marine resources and arable land has been an on-going indicators for conflict and assertive behaviour among the citizenry. Legislative measures are also a crucial pillar in preventing the spread of ideologies that encourages violence. The de-radicalisation processes amongst the returning fighters from conflict zones, require a robust legislative mechanism for rehabilitating of the individuals as well as their families. An effective legislature is also required to deal with those who are preaching, affiliating and funding the spread of radical ideologies as well as taking part in violent terror attacks.

Other fundamental element of countering the challenges posed by extremist ideologies is to empower and create awareness among the local communities who are vulnerable to recruitment or are exposed to terror networks. Community building and development projects could be a precursor to prevent the spread of radical ideologies among the persecuted and poverty-stricken communities. Periodical engagement and awareness of vulnerable communities are of utmost importance to ensure that every individual is aware of the dangers and threats of radicalisation. In these engagements, it would be important to involve the local community leaders, Islamic scholars and NGOs with the security and law enforcement agencies.

The spread of radicalisation also requires a well-coordinated approach between government and law enforcement agencies at the national, sub-regional, regional and at international levels. This should include capacity building, joint training, joint exercises and an information sharing mechanism that would provide uninterrupted and timely flow of intelligence on terror related activities.

Conclusion

World is facing one of the biggest challenges in countering radical ideology that is pushing youth to violent extremism. The prevention requires an inclusive approach to salvage the radicalised youths back to the mainstream. Each of the 37 littoral nations of the IOR are interconnected through culture and trade. Targeting the traditional trade routes and the shore facilities by transnational terrorists serve as feeding points for development and certainly require a regional approach.

The peace, prosperity and de-radicalisation entails a systemic approach to reduce the culture of violence in the IOR. Kinetic means are insufficient in countering such ideologies. Hence, it requires engagement with the communities, rehabilitation of de-radicalised youths and gainful employment of unemployed youths. De-radicalisation is a process laden with meticulous efforts by a number of agencies and require patience. It can be achieved through awareness and resilience at all levels. Role of civil society is as important as the government, hence civil society, government agencies and religious clerics must join together to help in de-radicalisation and rehabilitation of youths.

PART- III

Role of Technology & International Security Mechanisms in Countering Transnational Terrorism

9

Role of Niche Technologies in Combating Terrorism

Col Vu Cao Dinh

In recent years, there has been a rise in transnational terrorism , which is characterised by its subtle forms and serious consequences, like striking terror into people's hearts and minds. Terrorism has become a serious threat that undermines peace, security and stability not only of a nation, region but also of the whole world. Nowadays, terrorists can be grouped together, trained and equipped with new-age weapons. Terrorists are known to have exploited the technology much faster than security forces, thus, will always remain ahead of the states in the innovative use of technology. Consequently, the fight against transnational terrorism will become extremely challenging.

Applying niche technologies to combat terrorism is the need of the hour. These moves can be seen as necessary adjustments in order to respond to rapid changes[1] of transnational terrorism. This paper analyses the growing trends in using modern technologies, to conduct terrorist activities and the role of niche technologies in combating terrorism.

Growing Trends in Using Modern Technologies to Conduct Terrorist Activities

The threat from terrorism is evolving rapidly and has the potential to cause unprecedented loss of lives and properties. One of the popular approaches

---

1   Terrorists can now take advantage of technology to disperse leadership, training, and logistics not just regionally but globally. The combination of simple operations, which involve crude tools like knives or cars, increased communicative capacity, and high-tech weapons, has made terrorism a real threat to the masses.

that terrorists may take in the future is to launch cyber and even drone attacks on critical national infrastructure such as power grids, nuclear power plants, communication, transport, financial and healthcare systems, and so on. If these attacks occur, they will definitely throw countries into chaos, causing widespread disorder, undermining national industrial capability, seriously affecting national psyche, and even causing mental disorders. Given their access to the knowledge of information technology, terrorist organisations can mount attacks through the World Wide Web (WWW) to disrupt services and disable daily lives. They may also be assisted by state sponsored non-state actors and forces inimical to the nation.

Furthermore, international terrorist organisations are taking advantage of digital platforms to disseminate and spread violent extremist narratives at international platforms. The Internet, social networks and other means of communication have been used by these organisations to expand their narratives. These narratives are creating social and cultural fault-lines to create instability. More alarmingly, these narratives remain potent drivers of many local and international conflicts, which have caused death of tens of thousands of innocent people. This is also the way to induce and recruit supporters, advocate violent extremism and undermine the legitimacy and power of states.

Modern technologies also improve the operational effectiveness of terrorist organisations by enabling them to establish secure communication, and speedy transmission of Operational instructions without being intercepted. A new generation of 'Chat Applications' such as Telegram and WhatsApp provide end-to-end encryption, thus, making users' messages more secure and causes challenges for the law enforcement agencies to monitor and intercept them.

Advancements in technology is also contributing to the operational effectiveness of terrorist groups, most notably, in the use of Unmanned Aerial Vehicle (UAV) and autonomous weapon systems. The proliferation and easy access to off-the-shelf UAV technologies have enabled terrorist organisations to use relatively cheap UAVs for conducting surveillance, reconnaissance and attacks, thus making the protection of critical national infrastructure increasingly difficult for even those countries with scientific and technological potential and large military budget.

The Role of Niche Technologies in Combating Terrorism

In recent decades, countering terrorism is one of the most important missions of the international community. While advanced technologies are usually applied to military operations, they are also regarded as effective weapons in the fight against terrorism. Therefore, harnessing modern technologies to counter terrorism is of utmost significance.

Raising People's Awareness of Terrorist Prevention, Response, and Countering the Terror Funding

Terrorist organisations can only exist and operate if they are supported by societies or segments of the population. This support enables them to recruit new members, get financial assistance, hide themselves from security forces, and mount terrorist attacks. The 'Fourth Industrial Revolution', has allowed terrorist organisations to exploit the internet, and WWW for radicalisation, networking and execution of operations. Though states have been slow in exploiting social media for countering narratives of the terror organisations, however, a proactive approach is essential. Cooperation between the government and corporate companies such as Google, Facebook, YouTube, etc., is of significant importance, which plays a decisive role in countering violent extremist narratives on the internet and social networks.

Detecting and Preventing Terrorist Risks in Cyberspace Effectively from Afar.

Cyber infrastructure, information and communication technology are both targets and weapons of terrorists. Hackers who break into computer systems can introduce malicious software (computer viruses and worms) to vulnerable networks, deface websites, launch denial-of-service attacks and disable services. They can use web applications to contact and share information with each other, mount coordinated attacks, raise funds, and recruit new members. Dark Web in-fact can be used as 'virtual training camps' that provide instructions on bomb-making techniques and innovative method of terror attacks. To respond to this new form of terrorism, governments have invested a great deal of efforts into monitoring suspected websites. However, this method is not fool proof. Therefore, the only way out is the use of Artificial Intelligence (AI).

Better Control of Terrorists' Movement

After September 11 attacks against targets in the United States, many governments and international organisations seek to invest in producing 'smart' passports or identity cards to monitor intra-state and inter-state movement of their citizens. Accordingly, these 'smart' passports will require storage of Biometric Data of fingerprints, physical recognition, voice patterns, digital signatures and preferably DNA. The level of sophistication of these technologies will make it difficult for terrorists to conceal identities. Thus, movements of suspected terrorists will be monitored closely by security forces. Technologies such as 'smart' passports or identity cards are expected to be effective means to prevent and combat terrorism.

Collecting Information and Directing Guided Weapon Systems to Engage Targets.

In counter terrorism operations in many countries globally, electronic reconnaissance systems are no less important than sophisticated weapons and cruise missiles. Militaries of advanced countries have employed different types of airborne observation and reconnaissance systems, including reconnaissance satellites, UAVs, reconnaissance aircraft and helicopters to support counter terrorism operations. These modern weapon systems are used to conduct surveillance, reconnaissance and collection of information that helps to prevent surprise attacks by terrorist organisations on critical infrastructure and military bases. Apart from information collection, armed UAVs have also become lethal instrument to counter acts of terrorism

Countering Terror Funding

The focus should be to track terror funding through the Hawala network and digital currency. It has become extremely difficult to track digital currency, especially block chain currency. There is a need to optimally use AI to trace the digital signature of terror funding.

Securing People's Lives and Property and National Critical Infrastructure

Mitigating collateral damage when launching attacks on biological, chemical weapons storage sites of terrorist organisations. Though it is rare, but terrorist organisations possessing biological and chemical weapons cannot be ruled out. However, the use of conventional weapons to destroy these storage sites could lead to unforeseeable consequences because there are risks of leaking harmful substances into the environment. In view of the foregoing, there is a need to create a weapon system that can neutralise the impact of biological and chemical agents.

Improving the Ability to Protect National Critical Infrastructure Against Terrorist Attacks by Using UAVs

Terrorists would attempt both hard and soft kill of the critical infrastructure. It would require hardening of the target and keeping it beyond the reach of the terror organisations from the cyber and kinetic weapons. Destruction of Saudi Oil facilities was a case of militias using sophisticated systems by skilfully avoiding air defence grids on the ground and aerial surveillance. Thus, a cyber-shield and cyber spear are as important as air defence system for hard and soft kill of incoming hostile system.

Supporting the Investigation of Terrorist Attacks

After each terrorist attack, the issue that draws special attention is of law enforcement agencies, to investigate and bring to light the chief instigators and perpetrators of the attacks. These are usually very hard and time-consuming processes for investigators, especially, when the investigators have to cope with the difficulty of handling vast amount of information. However, thanks to the developments of high-tech tools and techniques for detecting evidence through using artificial intelligence[2] AI and DNA analysis, the investigation process will become easier and faster than before, contributing to revealing the real perpetrators of terror attacks. As for cyber-attacks, security experts now can use different types of software[3] to analyse the history of visited sites in browsers such as Google Chrome, Mozilla Firefox, Microsoft Edge, Internet Explorer, etc., to collect detailed information on suspects.

---

2   Tools and techniques for detecting evidence use artificial intelligence (AI) to locate objects in photos, taken at the scene of terrorist attacks, and relate them to previous cases. Given its ability to relate chains of complex evidence, AI is supporting investigators effectively.

3   These types of software programmes analyze contents of both existing and deleted browser system files and collect a user's online activities. The utilities allow investigators to analyze browsing history, social media messages, search history, emails, videos watched on YouTube, and so forth.

Facilitating the Training of Counterterrorist Forces

The training of counterterrorist forces is a vital task, which helps to ensure the effectiveness of counter terrorism in each country. Therefore, the application of advanced technologies, especially simulation technology, for training counterterrorist forces in the education and training institutions will facilitate the training process, enable learners to easily understand different scenarios and practise counterterrorist skills.[4] This is economical as well as contemporary to keep pace with the terror trends. The challenges of transnational terrorism are seen in various fields and are more complex in comparison with traditional security. Therefore, the prevention and response to these challenges require not only a synchronised, coherent combination of political, economic, diplomatic, legal, scientific and technological solutions, but also the choice of proper methods. Depending on specific circumstances, countries can decide to apply multiple measures to combat transnational terrorism. Military measures alone cannot address the root causes of terrorism in these fast-evolving situations.

Conclusion

The risks of transnational terrorism still persist and pose threat to nations across the globe. Transnational terrorism threatens peace and security in many regions and around the world. To effectively respond to the challenges of terror organisations using modern technologies, countries need to apply niche technologies in an appropriate manner. Use of modern technology as a weapon to deter, deny and destroy terror modules is the need of the hour. Thus, technology is required to deny and disable technologies of the terror organisations.

---

4   Simulation technology can be applied to create 3D digital models, which are used to simulate acts of a terrorist or terrorist group, acts of counterterrorist forces, scenarios of terrorist attacks and responses of security forces.

10

Role of Niche Technologies and Artificial Intelligence in Combating Terrorism: An Indian Perspective

Lt Gen (Dr) SP Kochhar
*AVSM**, SM, VSM (Retd)*

The emerging environment shows a rapid convergence of technology and terrorism, representing a feedback loop between the real and the virtual, in which cyberspace and emerging niche technologies are facilitating terrorist activities at an unprecedented scale. The innovations in digital technology and the proliferation of social media platforms have effectively flattened the intellectual battlefield and have given the tech-savvy groups the ability to wage war without the need for massive budgets. Increasingly, terrorist organisations are using a wide range of technologies as they plan and stage attacks.

The military must first understand not only the niche technologies, but also the purpose and way the technology is used. This should include use of weapons and how new technologies might increase the effect and casualties (fatal & non-fatal). It is also important to understand how technology is used for recruiting, information campaigns, information gathering, assessment, planning, coordination, logistics, and command and control - all of which play an important role in delivering the terrorist's weapon to its intended target with lethal impact. Therefore, the three main themes to counter the misuse of technology by transnational terrorists are:-

(a) The Nature of Threat: Use of Niche Technologies and Artificial Intelligence by Terrorists.

(b) Innovative Use of Niche Technologies to counter the threat from terrorists.

(c) Development of national, regional and international approaches and strategies.

Emerging Niche Technologies

Artificial Intelligence - New technologies are focused on augmenting the processing capabilities of machines for human-like intelligence (e.g., robotics, natural-language processing, and speech recognition). Technologies that fall under AI are machine learning, data science, robotics, internet of things and big data. Applications of AI - like image recognition, machine translations or music generation, are already launched. .

Additive Manufacturing - Additive Manufacturing or 3D printing refers to a production method whereby three-dimensional products are created by successively layering material, using a computerized or digital process. Drones and even weapon parts can be printed.

Augmented Reality - Augmented Reality (AR) is a form of technology used to provide a digitally enhanced view of the real world. This technology layers digital information (e.g., graphics, sound, or feedback) on top of the physical environment for the user to manipulate. It is useful for immersive training.

Automation - Physical objects are becoming more and more frequently interconnected with digital technology (e.g., advanced robotics and sensing) and able to communicate without human intervention.

Block Chain Systems - Block Chain systems use a distributed ledger technology to promote transparency, trust, and decentralized validation among members of the digital network.

Cloud Technology - Cloud Technology allows users to access scalable technology services immediately via the Internet's existing network, promoting lower infrastructure, inventory, and overhead costs, and creating leaps in computing power and speed, data storage, and bandwidth.

Crowd Sourcing - As consumers are increasingly interconnected through social media platforms, collective intelligence gathering is being leveraged to elicit perspectives and insights from a wide variety of individuals.

Data Mining, Link Analysis Technologies, Big Data and Data Visualization- Data Mining is a technology for analyzing historical and current online data to support informed decision making. The primary goals of data mining are prediction and description.

Digitisation- The proliferation of new mobile technologies, the rise of the Internet of Things (IoT), reliance on sensor and wearable technologies, and increased reliance on digital interaction has shifted the world from an analog to a digital one.

Do-It-Yourself (DIY) - Driven by the Internet and smart phones, individuals are increasingly engaging with the digital world to make purchasing decisions and perform tasks without professional assistance.

Drones – This can carry payloads of varying nature and be autonomous or command guided. Drones can be used for targeted strike, surveillance and electronic warfare. Range is dependent on size and endurance.

Geospatial Technology - The process of gathering and analyzing geographical data to understand the locational patterns of a subject has become prevalent. Much of satellite imagery can now be bought in the open market.

Communication Networks and Cyber - Network technologies consist of connectivity technologies (e.g., wireless routers), mobile computing (e.g., laptop computers), personal electronic devices (e.g., personal digital assistants and cell phones), IT services and Internet access, video recording. In addition, network technologies assist militaries in Command, Control, Communication, Computing, Intelligence, Surveillance, and Reconnaissance (C4ISR). Some features of the internet, like end-to-end encryption and Virtual Private Network (VPN) have made it useful for both security forces and terror organisations.

IoT - Electronic devices connected to the Internet that can be accessed remotely continues to grow (e.g., sensor technology, wearable technologies, connected vehicles).

Social Media - The rise of social media as a dominant platform for communication, has led to new forms of rapid connectivity and interaction across the global landscape. Social media also enables deniability and behaviour pattern of an individual because a user's identity can be concealed.

Use of Niche Technologies by Terrorists

Even when new technologies were emerging, the terrorists had continued to use low end technologies such as IEDs and mobile phones as tools of waging war. They were rarely seen to be using emerging technologies till the time these technologies became common place and affordable. They had used technologies that they are confident in and comfortable with. Any device or technology which has widespread use and permits near anonymous acquisition, training and maintenance is the one they prefer. This is a trend that will continue and the principles for adoption will remain 'Versatility, Variety, Efficiency, and Effectiveness'. The terrorist groups adopt a technology, if it can confer benefits with reasonable risks so as to improve the organization's ability to carry out activities relevant to its strategic objectives, such as:-

(a) Recruiting

(b) Acquiring resources

(c) Training

(d) Creating false identities, forgery, and other deception

(e) Reconnaissance and surveillance

(f) Planning and Targeting

(g) Communication

(h) Propaganda and persuasion.

Some of these technologies include :-

(a) Virtual Gaming Technology

(b) Cyber payment systems for fund transfer

(c) Massively multiplayer games for training

(d) Ubiquitous replication of high-quality forged credentials

(e) Impersonation of key persons in electronically mediated individual communication

(f) Worldwide, secure, multimode mobile data and voice communication

(g) Falsified video and audio avatars of leadership figures for public propaganda

(h) Electronic hijacking of news media outlets

(i) Echo chambers

(j) Social media

(k) Dark net and encrypted communications to share expertise, such as improvised explosive device (IED) designs and attack strategies, as well as to coordinate and facilitate attacks.

(l) Use of Artificial Intelligence for the following:-

  (i) Larger and more precise cyber-attacks, which can evade detection and overwhelm existing defences

  (ii) To generate high-quality fake videos or images - so called deep fakes

Self-hosted servers which are immune to takedowns, except by the web host, for example RocketChat, offer both cloud-hosting on its own servers and self-hosting. Some of these technologies include:-

(a) Those that improve the outcome of its attack operations. Even though drones were around much earlier, the terrorist groups used them only in 2014 for surveillance and in 2018 for attack.

(b) The terrorist groups are now adding cheap long-range autonomous weapons like powerful small warheads that can be set off by a fire and forget micro drone programmed with task specific AI engine. No command and control communication links may be necessary – making jamming ineffective.

(c) The components for assembling these technological implements and even small weapons can now be printed on an anonymous 3D printer which is easily available commercially and can be bought off the shelf without raising suspicion.

(d) Uses of network technology such as remote command detonation and sensor-initiated detonation of explosive devices, do offer improved attack capabilities to terrorists in several circumstances.

(e) Commercially available drones, self-driving cars or autonomous weapons systems could be reprogrammed, including connecting them to AI, so that terrorists can launch lethal attacks, release deadly materials in public areas, or carry out targeted killings.

(f) Other technological developments in the fields of AI, robotics technology, big data and biotechnology may also be misused to expand the range and lethality of their attacks.

Use of Technology by Defence to Counter Terrorist Groups

Security forces need to appreciate the enemy at all the three continuums of strategy, operational and tactical. This will result in clarity of options.

Assessing the Terrorist Groups Options

Data Analysts will carry out risk analysis for decision makers, under the following heads

(a) **Threat**- A data visualization enabled presentation of priorities to decision makers giving the following: -

   (i) Modus operandi

   (ii) Groups involved

   (iii) Trends and Predictions

   (iv) Locations

(b) **Vulnerability**- Capacity of deployed systems to mitigate the threat, taking into account-

   (i) Border Porosity

   (ii) Own preparedness including technical and Interoperability

(iii) Counter measures and Effectiveness.

(c) **Impact**- Scenario painting for getting results affecting the Military

(i)   Legal

(ii) Humanitarian

Techniques for Assessment

To conduct effective risk analyses, one will require databases from multiple agencies, duly collated for processing. These databases could come from inter agency or intra agency sources. Requires a 'Distributed Risk Analyses Network' to be established, spanning databases and overlaid with focused AI tools, Big Data, Machine Learning (ML), Data Link (DL), robotics, tagging using 'Information Grading', and predictive analytics which is modular and interoperable. Augmented Reality (AR), and Virtual Reality (VR), 'Gaming Theory' will draw data inputs for answers to questions like:-

(a) How have terrorists used niche and network technologies to support terrorist operations in the past, in the present, and how are they expected to use them in the future and what effects it will lead to?

(b) Identify which network and niche technologies were most attractive to terrorists and which would be most useful for a given terrorist activity, whether they would be practical to acquire, and whether any technologies might offer revolutionary changes.

(c) Assessment will be based on the expectation that terrorists will adopt a technology if it can confer one of two types of benefits mentioned above.

(d) Study about how terrorists acquire technologies.

(i)   Invest in specialized technology

(ii) Either rely on versatile technologies that can be used in many ways or pursue a wide variety of individual technologies, from legal or illegal market sources.

(iii) Use technology opportunistically.

The above will lead to approaches that the terrorists are likely to take, based on:

(a) The nature of the technology,

(b) The operational environment in which it would be useful,

(c) The general effect of its use, and the acquisition approach it requires. Above will lead to a simple model that can serve as a framework for evaluating the effectiveness of options for security forces, to respond to these general approaches to technology used by the terrorists.

Own Options

This requires assessing the benefits and risks of different countermeasure options that considers three basic factors:

(a) The role that a specific network technology plays within a terrorist group's overall technology strategy.

(b) The balance of benefits and risks of technology use, from both, the terrorists' and security forces' perspectives.

(c) Options for security forces to counter terrorists' use of network technologies.

Courses of Action

The options that emerge would be to:-

(a) **Deny** – Attempting to preclude terrorists from getting the types of technology they want will not be practical and developing direct counters to them will unlikely yield a high payoff.

(b) **Counter** - will require specialized efforts.

(c) **Exploit** – The best use of resources to counter terrorist operations would be to develop ways to exploit the technologies that terrorists will continue to use. As is the case with most people who use cell phones and computers, most terrorists do not have detailed knowledge of how those devices work. Therefore, it may be possible for sophisticated security forces to alter them in ways that enable security services to identify the users or their locations or to monitor their transmissions. This approach also targets a key vulnerability: an absolute need of terrorist organisations to remain hidden.

The situation at hand will finally decide what course would be best to follow within the time and space constraints.

Recommended Preparatory Actions.

Design a System to Address Terrorist Use of Network Technologies- Security organisations need a process that determines whether new network technology has been or is likely to be introduced into terrorist operations, identify its effect, select a response, gather needed resources, and implement an appropriate counter to the technology's use, and to do all of these in a timely manner.

Design an AI on Demand Platform- Need an AI-on-demand platform to facilitate sharing of new technologies and advances across domains. In addition, such a hub would serve as a common reference testing and experiment facility (could be a virtual network of physical facilities) to test state-of-the-art technology in the context of all the technical and non-technical constraints imposed by the field (economic, legal, structural, organisational). This hub could also include regulatory sandboxes, in order to test practical solutions in environments, where the regulatory context might need to be adapted or defined.

Exploit AI Technologies- Use this for cyber security operations, including the prevention, detection and response of cyber security incidents, through advance threat intelligence and predictive analytics on massive data, generated due to increased Internet use for terrorist purposes. For counter terrorism purposes, significant amount of knowledge about the functioning, activities and sometimes the targets of terrorist organisations are derived from website, chat room and other Internet communications.

Develop a Cyber and AI Range- A huge amount of up-to-date high-quality data is needed to develop reliable AI tools in support of cyber security and terrorism. This requires development of testing datasets at a national level for forecast, assessment of physical and cyber risks, prevention, detection and response, and, in case of failure, mitigation of consequences, and fast recovery after incidents.

Data Normalization over Cloud- Large amounts of data and information from a variety of origins and several formats have become available on different kinds of hardly interoperable displays. However, human cognitive is limited at managing information from several sources simultaneously and limits their ability to act. Furthermore, security forces often work in sparsely populated and remote areas where the availability of telecommunication networks may be an issue. Research and innovation should lead towards (cloud-based) integrated systems with simple but complete and highly-standardised interfaces, showing real-time information in a user-friendly way, which can assist in decision-making, and in remaining in contact with their command and control centers.

Research and Loop Back Techniques and Processes- The IoT can potentially connect practically everything, making everything more vulnerable. Wearable devices make us traceable, 3D printers can produce weapons, autonomous cars provide opportunities for kidnappers, teleworking opens doors for cyber-espionage etc. Terrorists are constantly seeking new ways to develop, deploy and activate dangerous chemicals (explosives, neurotoxins, new drugs, etc.)

Procurement Issues- The government moves slowly, devoting resources and training to problems as they become acute. In the short- and medium-term, however, the government often lacks capacity to manage a new challenge, especially technological, as the pace of change is so rapid. This allows terrorists freedom to exploit new developments as governments struggle to catch up.

International Cooperation and Sharing of Data as per UN Resolutions

Collaborative Response- It is also possible to combine non-lethal weapons with lethal ones or with electronic, psychological, and/or information warfare, making these other anti-terrorism tools more effective.

Acquire and sustain people with the core competencies needed, to make the system work- Security forces involved in combating terrorism need the following core competencies to address the use of technologies by terrorist organisations:

(a) An understanding of the technical challenges of exploitation and the operational limitations of the technologies themselves.

(b) An ability to track terrorist adoption, use, or avoidance of particular technologies.

(c) A capability to determine responses, which is most appropriate in light of security force goals.

(d) Capacity to develop plans and execute operations to actuate the selected responses to counter terrorist organisations.

Partnerships with Industry

Given the explosion in technologies, it is unrealistic for the government to have full-time employees who are experts on all of them. One way to mitigate this personnel problem is to expand partnerships outside government, drawing on individuals from the private sector, including start-ups suitably guided, where much of the expertise lies.

A 'Territorial Army Unit' that would bring in part-time embodied personnel with a technical background would expand the range of skills available to the government and increase private sector awareness of government needs. It would mitigate some of the problems the government faces, including salary disparities, strengthening surge and niche capacities, and improving the government's short-term responsiveness.

Conclusion

Terrorist groups have limited resources and limited means; thus, they are quick to refine their methods. Breaking the cycle of innovation and counter measures between terrorism and counter terrorism calls for unprecedented innovation with which terrorists cannot compete. Technology is not the only answer to addressing the spectre of transnational terrorism, and the technological answers we have today are inadequate to deal with the scope, and potential severity of the threat. Rather than adapting technologies to stay apace of evolving dangers and changing tactics, we need to get ahead of the terrorists. This requires vision and strategy, and a good strategy requires hard choices for the most crucial technological investments. These are:-

(a) **Seeking** technologies that can build a true national system that addresses all the challenges of terrorism from intelligence and early warning to domestic counter terrorism and response. Since no country will have the resources it needs to address every security shortfall, the first priority should be to invest in technologies that best leverage all the existing capabilities that are available by integrating them into a cohesive system.

(b) **Adopting** technologies that get the 'biggest bang for the buck.' Spending a little on many things may not buy much of anything. Targeting investments in the technologies that can provide the most security for the resources invested, as also are flexible, and contribute to addressing a wide range of threats, is a better approach.

(c) **Reaching** for 'breakthrough' technologies. Terrorist groups are quick to refine their methods, improve on techniques, improvise, and seek new ways to strike or attack new targets. Breaking the cycle of innovation and counter measures between terrorism and counter terrorism calls for unprecedented innovation, which terrorists cannot compete.

11

Threat from Chemical, Biological, Radiological and Nuclear (CBRN) Weapons

Dr Roshan Khanijo

Changing political environment and development of niche technologies have brought threats emerging from Chemical Biological Radiological Nuclear (CBRN) Weapons to the forefront. The use of Chemical Weapons in West Asia along with the usage of nerve gas in Europe, reinforces that the threat is still prevalent. There are treaties to control this threat like the Chemical Weapons Convention or (CWC), which aims to eliminate an entire category of weapons, by prohibiting the development, production, acquisition, stockpiling, retention, transfer or use of chemical weapons by States Parties[1]. Similarly, Convention on the Prohibition of the Development, Production and Stockpiling of Bacteriological (Biological) and Toxin Weapons and on their destruction, aims for the prohibition of the development, production and stockpiling of chemical and bacteriological (biological) weapons and their elimination, through effective measures[2]. For nuclear weapons also there are number of treaties like the International Atomic Energy Agency (IAEA), United Nations Security Council Resolution 1540, etc. However in spite of all these, the challenge to address the threat continues.

---

1 Chemical Weapons Convention, at https://www.opcw.org/chemical-weapons-convention

2 Convention on the Prohibition of the Development, Production and Stockpiling of Bacteriological (Biological) and Toxin Weapons and on Their Destruction, at http://disarmament.un.org/treaties/t/bwc/text

Chemical Weapon Threat

CWC defines the Chemical Weapons as those "Toxic Chemicals and their Precursors, or the Munitions and devices, specifically designed to cause death or other harm, through the toxic properties of those toxic chemicals, or any equipment specifically designed for use directly in connection with the employment of munitions and devices"[3]. Further, 'Toxic Chemicals' is defined as any chemical which through its chemical action on life processes can cause death, temporary incapacitation or permanent harm to humans or animals[4]. Different types of chemical agents which can be used are categorised under the following heads: -

(a) Nerve Agents- like- Tabun, Sarin, Soman Cyclosarin, Methyl phosphonothioic and can cause irreversible damage or death.

(b) Blister agents like Sulfur Mustard (Yperite), Nitrogen Mustard, Lewisite, phosgene Oximine can cause skin blistering, eye irritation and lung damage.

(c) Choking Agents like Phosgene, Diphosgene, Chlorine, and Chloropicrin can irritate the lungs and can be fatal.

(d) Central Nervous System (CNS) - acting agents can cause symptoms including paralysis and hallucinations. And some examples of this class are BZ, anaesthetics, and opioids.

(e) Blood Agents constitute Arsenic, Cyanide, etc. They are potentially fatal as they interfere with body's ability to use oxygen.

Since 1917, mustard gas has been used as a weapon. Mustard gas can be manufactured with ease and its vapor form is preferred in Chemical Warfare. Further the use of Sarin in Japan and other chemicals in the Syrian conflict demonstrate the capabilities of non-state actors to acquire these harmful chemicals. Similarly, the threat of biological weapons cannot be ignored.

---

3   Convention on the Prohibition of the Development, Production, Stockpiling and Use of Chemical Weapons and on their Destruction, at https://www.opcw.org/sites/default/files/documents/CWC/CWC_en.pdf

4   Ibid

Biological Weapon Threat

Biological weapons are complex systems that disseminate disease-causing organisms or toxins to harm or kill humans, animals or plants and mainly consist of two parts – a weaponised agent and a delivery mechanism[5]. Their use can vary from "Strategic or Tactical Military Applications, to political assassinations, the infection of livestock or agricultural produce to cause food shortages and economic loss, the creation of environmental catastrophes, and the introduction of widespread illness, fear and mistrust among the public"[6]. They also have various categories like:-

(a) Disease transmitted directly from person to person causing high mortality rates. The examples of this are Anthrax, Botullism, Plague, Smallpox, Tularemia

(b) Moderate morbidity rate as the disease is moderately easy to disseminate and cause low mortality rates. Examples are Glanders, Abrin, Epsilon, Brucella etc.

(c) Pathogens that can be mass disseminated, examples include H1N1 Influenza, HIV, Nipah Virus, Sars-Respiratory Disease, etc.

This has varied delivery mechanisms ranging from the wet form to the dry, and the aerosolized agents, thus, making the biological weapons more dangerous and difficult to control. The radiological and the nuclear weapons are another category where the threat though not common but quite feasible.

Radiological and Nuclear Weapon Threat

A "dirty bomb" is a type of "radiological dispersal device" (RDD) that combines a conventional explosive, such as dynamite, with radioactive material, though most RDDs would not release enough radiation to kill people or cause severe illness but can create fear and panic , whereas, the conventional explosive itself would be more harmful to people[7]. The damage caused will depend upon the type of radiation absorbed whether it is alpha,

---

5   What are Biological and Toxin Weapons"? at https://www.unog.ch/80256EE600585943/ (httpPages)/29B727532FECBE96C12571860035A6DB?OpenDocument

6   Ibid

7   Backgrounder on Dirty Bomb, USNRC, AT https://www.nrc.gov/reading-rm/doc-collections/fact-sheets/fs-dirty-bombs.html

beta or gamma rays, its amount, the distance and the time of exposure by an individual. The major challenge is to control the proliferation of the radioactive substance. Considering that these substances are used in commercial industries, hospitals and laboratories, so it is essential that a proper inventory both at the source as well as at the disposable levels is maintained. These substances though can be detected by equipment which generally the emergency responder carry, but the decontamination is a complicated process. Also, it is an expensive and time consuming work, and if the affected area is a financial hub then the activities in that region will be curtailed for quite some time, impacting the business, leading to financial losses.

Nuclear vulnerability can be either through the theft of the weapon/ fissile material, or through the sabotage of a commercial nuclear power plant. In the latter case, Cyber-attack is one of the major threats, as the terrorists may hack systems and disable cooling functions, which will be catastrophic for the plant. Further, the vulnerability to systems by infecting it with viruses cannot be ruled out as the terrorist with the help of an insider can easily get the access. The possibility of theft of nuclear weapon is remote, but nations like Pakistan are using Tactical Nuclear Weapons (TNW) where the weapons are delegated to the local commanders, so the vulnerability increases, as Pakistan is the hub of terrorist organisations.

International Organisations

Apart from the treaties mentioned in earlier paragraphs for countering the chemical and biological treaties a number of other treaties have been created with the aim to address all aspects of vulnerability. IAEA is the primary treaty for addressing nuclear related issues. Further, various other treaties like Convention for the Physical Protection of Nuclear Material (CPPNM) and 2005 Amendment, Convention for the Suppression of Acts of Nuclear Terrorism (ICSANT), United Nations Security Council Resolution 1540, Nuclear Suppliers Group (NSG), Fissile Material Cut-off Treaty (FMCT), Nuclear Security Summits etc have been formed periodically.

In spite of all these treaties one finds that there have been incidents where chemicals were used. Recently sarin, and chlorine gas, were used as a choking agent in Syrian conflict. Alleged use of chemical weapons by Daesh in Iraq, in 2017, the nerve agent OEthyl S2diisopropylaminoethyl methyl phosphonothiolate (VX) was used to assassinate Kim Jong Nam, and in 2018, Sergey Skripal and his daughter Yulia was poisoned with the Soviet-era nerve agent Novichok in UK. These are just a few contemporary examples.

Challenges

The fact that the threat still exists in spite of a plethora of treaties is a cause of concern. The reasons for this are as follows: -

(a) Treaties have a Limited Mandate.

(b) Veto Power prevents effective action against the hostile state, as attribution carries large political implications.

(c) Enforcement Mechanism and monitoring are weak, and reporting requirements are not well structured.

(d) Lack of synergy between the private chemical industry and security mechanisms. Private Industry remains a soft target for the terrorists.

(e) Digital security can be compromised through cyber-attack, vicious malwares and leakage of industrial gas remains a potent hazard.

(f) Advancements in nanotechnologies and bioengineering makes it difficult to counter certain threats emanating from these inventions.

(g) Development of the gene editing technique CRISPR-engineered versions of bacteria and viruses is a cause of concern.

(h) Easy availability of information in the field of synthetic biology.

(i) Cyber-attacks.

(j) Commercial Unmanned Aerial Vehicles (UAV) as a mechanism for carrying out acts of CBRN terrorism.

(k) 3D printing if accessed by non-state actors can increase the threat.

Way Forward

Prevention of the threat should be the first priority of any nation and for that one needs to enhance the security mechanism by developing strong intelligence network so that with timely input the threat can be prevented. Secondly, a systematic approach is required to detect and decontaminate the CBRN hazard. An effective training modules needs to be adopted especially at the grass root level. There should be synergy not only between the nations and international treaty organisations, but also between various national stake holders, especially between Central and State responders. One needs to integrate and standardize curriculum to suit the respective first responder. Thirdly, one must make use of the niche technologies especially for training purposes where one can use the computer-driven modelling simulators to create real time situations. In order to prevent the pilferage of chemical and biological agents, strong inventory checking system at the source as well as at the disposable level needs to be done. Further, one should involve the industry in highlighting security both in and around the complex. Finally, strict rules should be framed, executed and stringent punishments be given, for any violation by commercial industrial and medical institutions. In case of biological threat, one should have the public as well as private infrastructure to analyse the threat and develop antidotes at a faster speed.

The threat is becoming more real, hence, it is imperative that the nations' address the challenges through strong legal systems, adopt niche technologies, and share information as also take punitive actions against the culprits. Global cooperation without biases is paramount for addressing this menace.

12

Collaborative Security Mechanism to Deal with Transnational Terrorism

Shri Asoke Kumar Mukerji, IFS (Retd.)

Collaborative security mechanisms to deal with transnational terrorism are a priority to achieve 'zero tolerance' of terrorism.[1] To be effective, such mechanisms need to be universal, i.e. anchored in the United Nations (UN). The dominant role of non-state actors in transnational terrorism gives urgency to counter the activities of transnational terrorism, which are linked to more than one national jurisdiction. The increasing use of new information and communication technologies has added another dimension to this threat. Effective international cooperation holds the key to the success of collaborative security mechanisms. This paper looks at the effectiveness of the UN as the primary collaborative security mechanism to respond to this challenge.

Overview

The UN General Assembly (UNGA) provides a platform for negotiating legally binding frameworks for supporting inter-governmental security collaboration. The legal principle driving these legal frameworks for countering transnational terrorism revolves around the principle of 'prosecute or extradite.' This principle enables countries impacted by transnational terrorism to investigate, prosecute and penalize alleged terrorists who may be located in different foreign jurisdictions.

---

1. United Nations, UNSC Meetings, SC/10447 dated 14 November 2011. Available at https://www.un.org/press/en/2011/sc10447.doc.htm

The UN Security Council (UNSC) has been given 'Primary Responsibility' by Article 24 of the UN Charter to maintain international peace and security. Due to Article 25 of the UN Charter, under which all member-states of the UN have agreed to implement UNSC decisions, these have a legally binding dimension. Countering terrorism has been an integral part of the UNSC's agenda since the late 1990s. The UNSC is the world's most important collaborative security mechanism to respond to transnational terrorism. Unlike the UNGA legal framework, the UNSC has the power to invoke measures under Chapter 7 of the UN Charter to enforce its resolutions to counter transnational terrorism.

Today, transnational terrorism is visible in Asia, Africa, Europe and the Americas. Regional bodies like the Shanghai Cooperation (SCO), the ASEAN Defence Ministers' Meeting (ADDM), the North Atlantic Treaty Organisation (NATO) and the Organisation of African Unity (OAU) have created collaborative regional security mechanisms to respond to the challenge of transnational terrorism. With a focus on their core regional membership, the growing international linkages between regions impacted by transnational terrorism has motivated several of these regional bodies to seek coherence with UN initiatives. This growing synergy is reflected by the increased interaction between the UNSC and these regional bodies in countering transnational terrorism.

Two norm-setting non-UN entities are being gradually integrated into the UNSC's attempts to counter transnational terrorism. These are the 37-country Financial Action Task Force (FATF), anchored in the Organisation for Economic Cooperation and Development (OECD), and the 29-country Global Counter Terrorism Forum (GCTF) sponsored by the United States.

An assessment of how effective the UN's collaborative security mechanisms have been to counter transnational terrorism reveals inherent limitations, which are linked to the way the UN organs are structured. As transnational terrorism takes advantage of the increasing inter linkages between member-states, propelled by the new technologies of the 21st century, the time has come to integrate existing UN initiatives to counter this threat into a multi-stakeholder process.

The UN General Assembly (UNGA)

Since 1972, the UNGA has sought to provide a legal framework through negotiating legal obligations of member-states which are codified in UN treaties and conventions on countering transnational terrorism. This approach of the UNGA mirrors the pre-Second World War legal initiative taken by France in 1937 that resulted in the adoption of a Convention for the Prevention and Punishment of Terrorism. India was among the 24 member-states of the League that signed the Convention, and the only member-state to have ratified it in 1941. The primary objective of the Convention was to seek the prosecution or extradition of the terrorists, alleged to have assassinated the King of Yugoslavia and the Foreign Minister of France at Marseilles in 1934.[2] The Convention has failed to deliver on this objective, as the country hosting the alleged terrorists, Italy, refused to cooperate.

Convened after the killing of Israeli athletes participating at the Munich Olympics in 1972, the UNGA had adopted a resolution on countering terrorism at its 27th Session.[3] This resolution created an Ad Hoc Committee to recommend the way forward. The Committee consisted of 35 member-states, including India. It submitted its recommendation in 1979, when India was its Chair, proposing the negotiation of an additional international convention, or conventions, based *inter alia* "on the principle of extradition or prosecution to combat acts of international terrorism not yet covered by other similar international conventions".[4]

Between 1979 and 1997, however, the UNGA failed to make any significant progress on implementing this recommendation. In 1997 the UNGA established an Ad Hoc Committee on Measures to Eliminate International Terrorism, open to all member states, through another unanimous UNGA Resolution.[5] The mandate given to the Committee

---

2   World Digital Library, "Convention for the Prevention and Punishment of Terrorism" 1937. Available at https://www.wdl.org/en/item/11579/

3   The United Nations, UN General Assembly Resolution 3034 dated 18 December 1972. Available at http://www.un.org/en/ga/search/view_doc.asp?symbol=A/RES/3034(XXVII)

4   The United Nations, UN General Assembly Official Records: Thirty Fourth Session, Supplement No. 37 (A/34/37), A/AC.160/SR.11-19, paragraph 118. Dated 17 April 1979.

5   The United Nations, UN General Assembly Resolution A/RES/51/210 dated 16 January

was to draft international legal instruments to counter terrorist bombings, suppress acts of nuclear terrorism, and develop "a comprehensive legal framework of conventions dealing with international terrorism".[6] A Declaration annexed to this Resolution placed emphasis on the principle of extraditing or prosecuting perpetrators of terrorist acts.[7]

It was in the context of discussions in the UNGA during this session that India took the lead to distil the discussions in the UNGA into a 'first draft' of a proposed CCIT.[8] The main objective of the proposed CCIT was the legal obligation on member-states to prosecute or extradite individuals located within their national jurisdictions who were alleged to have committed terrorist acts in foreign jurisdictions. However, for over 20 years, the UNGA has not succeeded in negotiating and adopting the CCIT. This has become a vulnerability in the UNGA's international legal architecture for successfully countering transnational terrorism.

The UN Security Council (UNSC)

The UNSC has adopted a 'robust' approach in enforcing UNSC resolutions to counter terrorism. It has relied on the enforcement provisions of Chapter 7 of the UN Charter to achieve this objective. Over 50 UNSC counter terrorism resolutions have been adopted over the past three decades. Despite this, it is apparent that the UNSC's 'robust' approach has not been able to effectively respond to the challenge posed by transnational terrorism.[9] This is due to the way in which the UNSC works, particularly the internal dynamics of relations between its five permanent members. This is illustrated by four examples.

First, UNSC Resolution 1267, adopted in 1999, had specifically proposed measures to counter transnational terrorism represented by

---

1997. http://www.un.org/en/ga/search/view_doc.asp?symbol=A/RES/51/210.

6   Ibid. See paragraph 9.

7   Ibid. See especially paragraphs 5-7 of the Declaration attached to the Resolution.

8   Letter from Permanent Representative of India to UN Secretary General dated 1 November 1996, UN Doc. A/C.6/51/6. This was subsequently revised in August 2000. Available at https://www.legal-tools.org/doc/f4d47d/pdf/

9   For a full listing of UNSC resolutions on countering terrorism, see Security Council Report, "UN Documents for Terrorism: Security Council Resolutions", 2019. Available at https://www.securitycouncilreport.org/un_documents_type/security-council-resolu tions/?ctype=Terrorism&cbtype=terrorism

the activities of Al-Qaeda and associated individuals and entities. This terrorist entity has been projected as the most active and widespread transnational terrorist network today. The Preamble of UNSC Resolution 1267, recalled obligations of parties to 'existing' international counter-terrorism conventions to "extradite or prosecute terrorists".[10] However, subsequent UNSC resolutions like the Omnibus Resolution 1373 (adopted unanimously after the 9/11 terror attacks of 2001 on the United States), do not refer at all to any obligation of member states of the UN to extradite or prosecute perpetrators of terrorist acts.[11] This impact adversely, on enforcing legal obligations of member-states to counter transnational terrorism on the basis of UNSC resolutions.

In September 2014, faced with growing evidence of the rapid spread of terrorism and the movement of terrorists across borders, the UNSC had adopted Resolution 2178 on "foreign terrorist fighters".[12] Paragraph 6 of this Resolution refers to the need for member states to 'prosecute and to penalize' terrorists. It omits the legal obligation on member states to do so, since the UNGA has no comprehensive convention on countering terrorism that requires prosecution or extradition of alleged terrorists.[13]

Second, there have been divergences between UNSC resolutions and UNGA Conventions on countering transnational terrorism. The case of UNSC Resolution 1540, adopted in 2004[14] to deal with the proliferation of weapons of mass destruction is relevant in this context. The resolution does not incorporate obligations to extradite or prosecute, although the International Convention on Suppression of Acts of Nuclear Terrorism which was adopted by the UNGA in 2005, imposes obligations on member states for the prosecution or extradition of perpetrators of terror acts.[15]

---

10 United Nations, UN Security Council Resolution 1267 dated 15 October 1999. Available at https://www.undocs.org/S/RES/1267%20(1999)

11 https://documents-dds-ny.un.org/doc/UNDOC/GEN/N01/557/43/PDF/N0155743.pdf?OpenElement

12 United Nations, UNSC Resolution 2178, dated 24 September 2014. Available at https://documents-dds-ny.un.org/doc/UNDOC/GEN/N14/547/98/PDF/N1454798.pdf?OpenElement

13 Ibid. Paragraph 6.

14 United Nations, UNSC Resolution 1540, dated 28 April 2004. Available at http://www.un.org/en/ga/search/view_doc.asp?symbol=S/RES/1540(2004)

15 United Nations, International Convention for the Suppression of Acts of Nuclear Terrorism, 2005. Available at https://treaties.un.org/doc/db/Terrorism/english-18-15.

This divergence is inexplicable, given the role of the permanent members of the UNSC as an 'institutional databank' of the Council.

Third, the integrity of the UNSC as a collaborative security mechanism to counter transnational terrorism has been impacted by its overtly political orientation on counter terrorism. Political approaches have diluted the obligations for collaborative security measures imposed on member-states to implement such resolutions. Even the uniform application of UNSC sanctions on terrorists and/or terrorist entities in the UNSC sanctions regimes,[16] which functions under an Ombudsman in the case of UNSC resolution 1267, has been impacted by this 'political' approach. India's request to the UNSC to list Masood Azhar provides a relevant case study of this phenomenon.[17]

Fourth, the policy of the UNSC on Afghanistan illustrates the limitations of using collaborative security mechanisms like the UNSC to counter transnational terrorism effectively. The UNSC divided Resolution 1267 in 2011 into two separate UNSC Resolutions (UNSC Resolution 1988 to focus on the Taliban and UNSC Resolution 1989 to focus on Al-Qaida). This was done at the instigation of the five permanent members of the UNSC to provide political flexibility to reintegrate elements of the Taliban listed earlier with Al-Qaida terrorists under UNSC Resolution 1267 into the political Afghan peace process.[18] This approach has made the UNSC ineffective in preventing the ongoing widespread terrorist activity in Afghanistan, which is characterized by its transnational character.

---

pdf. Articles 10, 11, 13 and 16 of the Convention deal with prosecution or extradition.

16   The uneven manner in which UNSC sanctions have been applied may be seen in a non-governmental report on this subject. Available athttp://www.securitycouncilreport. org/atf/cf/%7B65BFCF9B-6D27-4E9C-8CD3-CF6E4FF96FF9%7D/special_research_ report_sanctions_2013.pdf

17   "Four fault-lines in Masood Azhar's UN listing" by Gautam Chikermane, Raisina Debates, Observer Research Foundation, New Delhi. 2 May 2019. Available at https://www.orfonline.org/expert-speak/4-faultlines-masood-azhar-un-terrorist-listing-50454/

18   United Nations, UN Security Council Resolution 1988, dated 17 June 2011. Available at https://www.undocs.org/S/RES/1988(2011)

The UN Secretariat

The ambitious UN Global Counter Terrorism Strategy (GCTS) adopted on 8 September 2006 [19] has four pillars, viz. Addressing conditions conducive to the spread of terrorism; preventing and combating terrorism; building States' capacity and strengthening the role of the UN; and ensuring human rights and the rule of law. All four pillars are relevant for countering transnational terrorism.

Collaborative security mechanisms of UN member-states have been institutionalized by the UN and provided with a permanent secretariat to ensure monitoring and implementation of decisions adopted by UN member-states. Under the GCTS, a Counter-Terrorism Implementation Task Force (CTITF) of the UNGA is meant to coordinate the work of more than 30 UN bodies and entities involved in countering terrorism.

The regular reviews of the GCTS by the UNGA have shown the uneven implementation of its four pillars. For example, given the importance of the principle of prosecuting or extraditing transnational terrorists through international cooperation, there has been no progress in adopting the CCIT which is listed under Pillar 4 so far. Instead, the main outcome of the work of the CTITF so far has been on capacity building in UNGA member-states, which is not the most important priority for countering transnational terrorism.

The UNSC has created a Counter-Terrorism Committee through UNSC resolution 1373 after the 9/11 terror attacks on the United States. A Counter Terrorism Executive Directorate (CTED) has functioned as a secretariat to help foster collaborative activity among UNSC member-states to implement counter-terrorism priorities, including on transnational terrorism.[20] However, the CTED works under the strict control of the five permanent members, whose veto power ensures that the political rather than legal dimension of countering such terrorism through the rule of law prevails.

---

19 United Nations, UN General Assembly Global Counter Terrorism Strategy. Available at https://www.un.org/counter terrorism/ctitf/en/un-global-counter-terrorism-strategy

20 United Nations, UNSC Counter Terrorism Committee. Available at https://www.un.org/sc/ctc/about-us/

Norm-Setting on Countering Transnational Terrorism

Faced with the ineffectiveness of the UN to provide specific outcomes in the area of norms for countering transnational terrorism, the role of two non-UN bodies in setting such norms has become prominent. By integrating their norms into the text of UNSC resolutions on countering terrorism, the UNSC has 'outsourced' its legal responsibility to set international norms for collaborative security to counter transnational terrorism to these two bodies.

The Financial Action Task Force (FATF)

One area is setting international norms on terror financing. The UNGA had adopted the legal framework in 1999 with the International Convention for the Suppression of Financing of Terrorism. All the five permanent members of the UNSC are members of FATF.

The lead in setting norms to counter terror financing has been taken by an inter-governmental organisation established by the G-7 Summit held in Paris in 1989 to tackle money laundering. The body, designated as the FATF, is serviced by the secretariat of the Organisation for Economic Cooperation and Development (OECD) in Paris.[21] India joined the FATF in 2010.

Following the 9/11 terror attacks on the United States; the FATF has added nine specific recommendations to counter the financing of terrorism.[22] The UNSC had earlier incorporated anti-terror financing provisions into UNSC Resolution 1267 adopted in 1999 to counter the terrorist threat posed by Al Qaida and the Taliban. Subsequently, FATF's Recommendations have been referred in the following UNSC counter terrorism resolutions: UNSC Resolution 1373 adopted after the 9/11 terror attack on the United States in 2001; UNSC Resolution 1540 adopted in 2004 on non-proliferation of weapons of mass destruction; UNSC Resolution 1718 adopted in 2006 on non-proliferation and the DPR of Korea, as well as UNSC Resolution 1737 adopted the same year on non-proliferation. Of the FATF Recommendations on international cooperation, Recommendation

---

21 The Financial Action Task Force (FATF), "Members and Observers", 2019. Available at .http://www.fatf-gafi.org/about/membersandobservers/

22 Ibid. "The FATF Recommendations", 2019. Available at http://www.fatf-gafi.org/ publications/fatfrecommendations/documents/fatf-recommendations.html

39 upholds the principle of either extraditing or prosecuting perpetrators of terrorism financing.

The FATF has assumed prominence in the past few years because of the way it has pursued the objective of compelling member-states of the UN to uphold their obligations under UNSC resolutions on sanctioning the financing of terror by individuals and groups. In India, the best-known example of the FATF's impact has been the scrutiny of Pakistan by the FATF to enforce UNSC resolutions.

Enforcement of FATF recommendations is through the conventional FATF route which uses international collaboration between inter-governmental bodies and commercial financial institutions, including banks. So far, this has proved to be an effective enforcement mechanism, illustrating the gradual effectiveness of a multi-stakeholder approach to countering global terror financing. An emerging alternative option is to use the UNSC resolutions, enforceable under Chapter 7 of the UN Charter. However, for reasons given earlier, until the UNSC is reformed to make its decisions implementable on the ground, this option may not be effective.

Global Counter Terrorism Forum (GCTF)

The second area is in international norm-setting for civilian efforts to counter transnational terrorism, including countering violent extremism and dealing with foreign terrorist fighters. Since 2011, a group of 29 countries have worked outside the UN to produce a body of such norms, which are gradually being integrated into the UNGA's implementation of its Global Counter Terrorism Strategy (2006) as well as into UNSC's resolutions to convert them from being 'best practices' into becoming enforceable norms.

The 29-country grouping is the Global Counter Terrorism Forum (GCTF), which was created by the United States in 2011.[23] The origin of the GCTF goes back to the Counter Terrorism Action Group (CTAG), established by the G8 Summit in Evian, France in 2003, as a reaction to the way the UNSC was countering terrorism.[24]

---

23 Global Counter Terrorism Forum, "Background and Mission", 2019. Available at https://www.thegctf.org/About-us/Background-and-Mission

24 Centre on Global Counter terrorism Cooperation, "The G8's Counter Terrorism Action Group" by Eric Rosand, May 2009. Available at https://www.ciaonet.org/attachments/14523/uploads

All five Permanent Members of the UNSC are members of the GCTF. The GCTF's Rabat Memorandum on 'Good Practices for Effective Counter Terrorism Practice', in the Criminal Justice Sector deals with the issue of extradition. Good Practice 9 calls for international cooperation, including extradition, but does not refer to the principle of "extradite or prosecute".[25] The GCTF is currently looking at using the criminal justice system to counter linkages between terrorism, transnational organized crimes and international crimes. Interestingly, not only the Good Practices for Effective Counter Terrorism Practice, but the entire corpus of the normative work done by the GCTF so far, has been incorporated into the UNSC Resolution 2178 on foreign terrorist fighters.[26]

Impact of Digital Technologies

As the world embraces digital technologies, the cyber dimension of collaborative security to counter transnational terrorism has become a priority.

The security of cyberspace has been prioritised by the UNGA through the work done to develop cyber security norms through a Governmental Group of Experts (GGE).[27] The scope of the GGE is limited by the mandate of the First Committee of the UNGA, which is focused on disarmament and the obligations of states for securing cyberspace. The activities of non-state actors in cyberspace pose a new challenge to collaborative security mechanisms to counter transnational terrorism.

As political polarization among the five permanent members of the UNSC restricts the implementation of the GGE outcomes, multinational corporations like Microsoft[28] have taken the lead in proposing international cooperation to address cyber security. These proposals from the corporate sector look to governments to create mechanisms for securing cyberspace.

---

25 Global Counter Terrorism Forum, "Rabat Memorandum"2012. Available at https://www.thegctf.org/Portals/1/Documents/Framework%20Documents/A/GCTF-Rabat-Memorandum-ENG.pdf?ver=2016-09-01-115828-653

26 United Nations, UNSC Resolution 2178, 24 September 2014. Available at https://www.undocs.org/S/RES/2178%20(2014)

27 United Nations, Office of Disarmament Affairs. "Developments in the field of information and communications in the context of international security", 2019. Available at https://www.un.org/disarmament/ict-security/

28 Microsoft, "A Digital Geneva Convention to protect Cyberspace". Available at https://query.prod.cms.rt.microsoft.com/cms/api/am/binary/RW67QH

The UNGA will need to initiate multi-stakeholder discussions leading to the negotiation of an enforceable International Convention on Cyberspace to respond to these emerging threats.

Conclusion

As this brief assessment has brought out, the overall situation regarding collaborative security mechanisms to counter transnational terrorism has been a cause for concern. The UNGA needs to prioritise the adoption of the CCIT to make international cooperation in countering transnational terrorism obligatory, under international law. The UNSC needs to be reformed, as mandated by world leaders at the 60th Anniversary Summit of the UN in 2005, to "enhance its effectiveness and the legitimacy and implementation of its decisions".[29] The emerging dimension of cyberspace in transnational terrorism needs to be integrated into the UN's work through multi-stakeholder participation to respond effectively to this significant international threat.

---

29   United Nations, UN General Assembly Resolution A/RES/60/1 dated 16 September 2005, paragraph 153. Available at https://www.un.org/en/development/desa/population/migration/generalassembly/docs/globalcompact/A_RES_60_1.pdf

PART- IV

Major Takeaways from the Panel Discussion

13

Countering Bio Organisms through Natural Plant Extracts

Shri Amul S Bahl

A bio-organism, in Collins Dictionary, is defined as "a dangerous fast-proliferating organism that could be used as the basis of a biological weapon".[1] These bio-organisms, in the form of bacteria, viruses, spores, act as the payload in a bio-terror attack. They become bio-agents. Transforming these bio-organisms through a cocktail mixture or making them more lethal and harmful by increasing their ability to cause disease, spread, and/or to resist medical treatment on a large uncontrollable scale is what makes them bio-agents.[2]

Medical science has solutions to various diseases caused by these microbes. Antibiotics are one of the important treatment lines in modern medicine towards combating infections and providing a cure.[3] However, antibiotic resistance among microbes is a serious global concern.[4] There is also a simultaneous concern of microbe mutations which result in antibiotic resistance.[5] Antibiotic resistant bacteria resulted in at least 2

1 https://www.collinsdictionary.com/dictionary/english/bio-organism. Accessed 22 November 2019.

2 https://medlineplus.gov/biodefenseandbioterrorism.html#cat_59. Accessed 11 November 2019.

3 Aslam, B. et al. Antibiotic resistance: a rundown of a global crisis. Infection and Drug Resistance, 2018, 11, 1645-1658.

4 Zaman, S. B. et al. A review on antibiotic resistance: alarm bells are ringing. Cureus, 2017, 9(6), 1403-1411.

5 Li, B. & Webster, T. J. Bacteria Antibiotic Resistance: New Challenges and Opportunities

million infections and 23,000 deaths a year, resulting in $ 55 to 70 billion per year economic impact in the United States alone.[6]

On one hand, these bio-organisms can cause various diseases in natural way but on the other hand they can be the cause of bioterrorism. The specter of a bio-terror may become larger than life due to the subversive activities in the backyard, rogue nations and disgruntled scientists in possession of these bio-organisms. Bioterrorism is a term referred to intentional use of pathogenic strains of microbes to cause disease or death in living entities and/or to cause harm to environment.[7] There are threats of bioterrorism, for example: the outbreak of pneumonic plague in Surat and bubonic plague in Beed in 1994 put India's defense and intelligence units on alert.[8] Bioterrorism is a worldwide concern. An example is the powdered anthrax spores, which were placed in letters mailed through the U.S. postal system in 2001, where 12 mail handlers suffered and five died.[9] Since 2001, the U.S. Government has made significant efforts towards responding to acts of bio-terror.[10] Often whether the spread of bio agents is natural or accidental or deliberate is difficult to ascertain. However, bio attack today is a Global threat.

There are a large number of agents which can be used for bioterrorism and are categorized in three categories (Figure 1); viz. category A, B and C.[11] Figure 2 presents the risk attributes for these three categories.

---

for Implant-Associated Orthopaedic Infections, Journal of Orthopaedic Research. 2018 January, 36(1), 22–32.

6   ibid.

7   Erenler, A. K., Güzel, M. & Baydin, A. How prepared are we for possible bioterrorist attacks: an approach from emergency medicine perspective. Hindawi The Scientific World Journal, 2018. https://doi.org/10.1155/2018/7849863

8   Sharma, R. India wakes up to threat of bio-terrorism. British Medical Journal, 323 September, 2001, 714.

9   https://www.cdc.gov/anthrax/bioterrorism/index.html.Accessed 11 November 2019.

10 National Strategy for Countering Biological threats. National Security Council, The White House, Washington, 2009, November. https://www.hsdl.org. Accessed 03 November 2019.

11 Erenler, Güzel, & Baydin, *op.cit.*

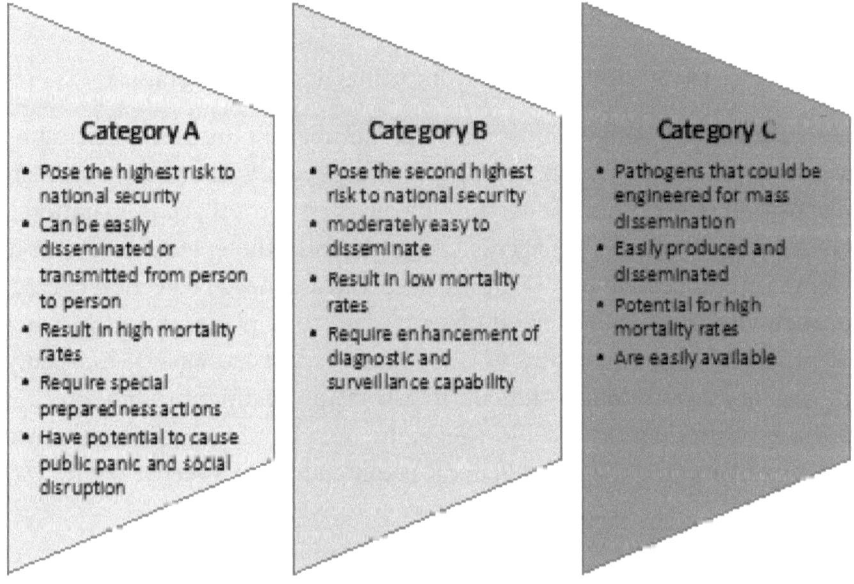

Figure 1: Categories of agents used in bioterrorism

Figure 2: Risk attributes of Category A, B and C agents

The risks (Figure 3) from bio agents, causing spread of diseases or the possibility of using them in bioterrorism can result in health, economic and strategic losses for the individuals, society and a nation.

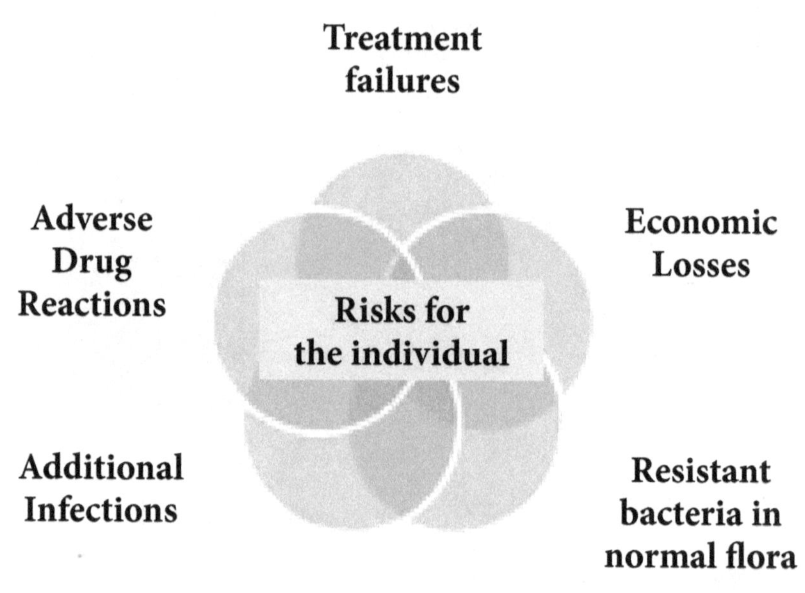

Figure 3: Possible risks to living beings due to bio-organisms

These bio-agents can spread via number of mediums including air, water, in food or even from person to person.[12] There is most likely disposition of these bio-agents through air as an aerosolized preparation.[13] Spread of pathogenic bio agents can go beyond the epicentre of origin. Communities need to be aware of such spread and need protection in cases of such attacks, like the spread of swine flu[14] took place beyond its place of origin. A high possibility of cocktail spread of bio agents, especially, in case of bioterrorism is difficult to ascertain, treatment of bio attack is difficult, as, to identify the bio-agents due to a combination of unknown bio-organisms and their interactions, is difficult. Such a scenario goes way

---

12   https://medlineplus.gov/biodefenseandbioterrorism.html#cat_59. *op.cit.*

13 White, S. M. Chemical and biological weapons. Implications for anaesthesia and intensive care. British Journal of Anaesthesia, 2002, 89 (2), 306-324.

14   Davis, C. P. & Stoppler, M. C. Swine Flu, 2019, WebMD https://www.emedicinehealth.com/swine_flu/article_em.htm. Accessed on 15 November 2019.

beyond an epidemic and requires emergent and drastic measures akin to disaster relief. In other words, multiple vectors need to be addressed concurrently.

Keeping in mind the fatal effects of bio-organisms as a national as well as Global threat, the objective of this paper is to present a solution called Whiff Bio-Spray as a bio defence in neutralizing the effects of bio organisms for health care, as well as to counter bioterrorism anywhere in the world.

Whiff Bio-Spray has been designed on the QLEN Model of disaster relief developed by the author. The QLEN Model when applied to Whiff Bio-Spray (Figure 4) is as follows:

(a) **Quick** - mobile solutions hence quick response; also quick acting once sprayed.

(b) **Localization** - confine infection to an area; avoid spread: Whiff Bio-Spray acts quickly to confine to a localized area thereby, blunting the lethality of spread of bio-organisms.

(c) **Elimination** - of bio-organisms

(d) **Neutralization** - of the bio-organism/terror threat

Quick Acting and Quick Response: It acts in minutes to neutralize bio-agents and thus, can save precious human lives from being infected or dead. It also arrests the spread of bio-organisms at a fast pace.

Mobility: There is no requirement of huge capital expenditure or fixed equipment to spread Whiff Bio-Spray in the area under bio-attack. It can be deployed quickly and effectively at any place. In large open areas, low flying drones can be effectively used to spread Whiff Bio-Spray.

Note: Concentration levels of bio-agent where levels 1, 2 and 3 mean

Level 1 – Maximum concentration, Level 2 = Medium concentration, Level 3 = Low concentration.

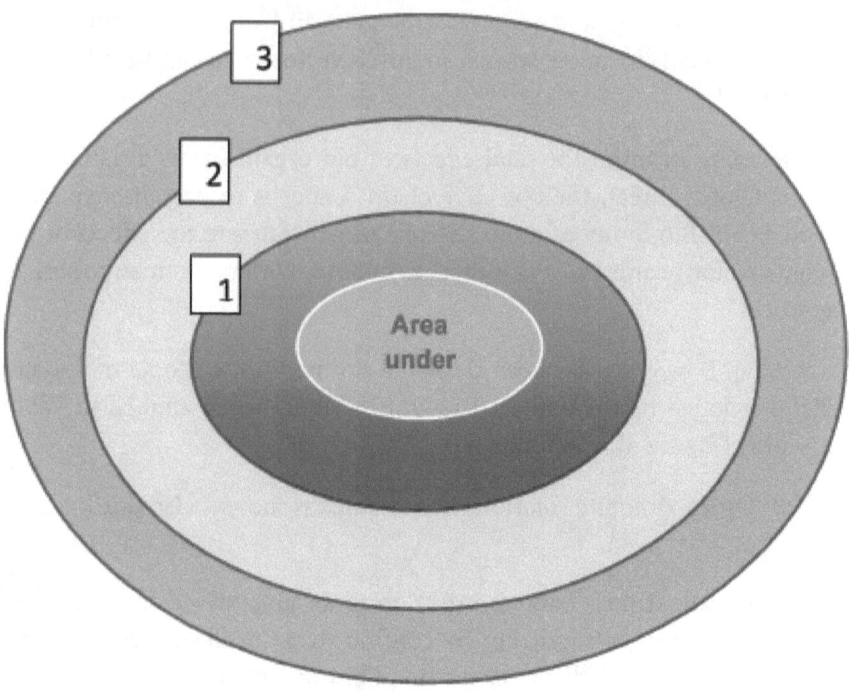

Figure 4: Whiff Bio-Spray at three concentration levels of pathogenic bio-agents to counter and neutralize a bio-attack.

Comprehensive Elimination of Broad Spectrum of Pathogenic Payload: Whiff Bio-Spray is effective to eliminate a broad spectrum of pathogens and viruses and thus, can effectively counter and neutralize a cocktail kind of bio-attack. As a strategy to counter a bio attack efficiently and effectively, Figure 4 illustrates a way of using Whiff Bio-Spray. It can be sprayed at three concentration levels not only to counter bio-organisms in the affected area but also to manage the spread of bio-organisms in adjacent areas to neutralize the bio terror threat and effect.

In other words, it will prevent proliferation of bio-organisms from the area under bio attack to surrounding areas. Further to use bio-spray at three concentration levels, there is need to look at the wind direction and wind speed to let bio-spray float with air along bio-organisms.

This QLEN approach helps in achieving the objectives mentioned in a key U.S. Government report - *"A National Blueprint for Bio defence: Leadership and Major Reform Needed to Optimize Efforts".*[15] It helps towards the mission of the Federal Government during a biological incident which is to:

(a) Save lives.

(b) Reduce human suffering.

(c) Protect property and the environment.

(d) Control the spread of disease.

(e) Support community efforts to overcome the physical, emotional, environmental and economic impacts.

A Solution to Bio-organisms: Whiff Bio-Spray

Whiff Bio-Spray and its Functioning

In ancient Vedic literature, it is indicated that active phytochemical constituents of individual plants can be used to form a polyherbal formulation for therapeutic effects.[16]Plant-extract oils have antibacterial and antifungal activities, and can also overcome problems of antibiotic resistance.[17]

Within the realm of Ayurvedic medicinal benefits, the author has developed a technological breakthrough (Figure 5 and Figure 6) using plant-based extracts which is a simple, safe and effective herbal solution (referred as 'Whiff Bio-Spray' in this paper) to counter bio-agents. It is a 100 percent natural spray of herbal extracts with no side effects and no ecological fallout. The herbal contents of the bio-spray float in the air, neutralizing bio-agents (Figure 5).

---

15 A National Blueprint for Biodefense: Leadership and Major Reform Needed to Optimize Efforts, 2015, October. https://s3.amazonaws.com/media.hudson.org/20151028ANATI ONALBLUEPRINTFORBIODEFENSE.pdf. Accessed on 14 November 2019.

16 Parasuraman, S., Thing, G. S. & Dhanaraj, S. A. Polyherbal formulation: Concept of Ayurveda. Pharmacognosy Review, 2014, July-December, 8(16), 73-80.

17 Priti, V. Use of essential oils against gram negative pathogens. Journal of Drug Delivery and Therapeutics, 2012, 2(6), 134-137.

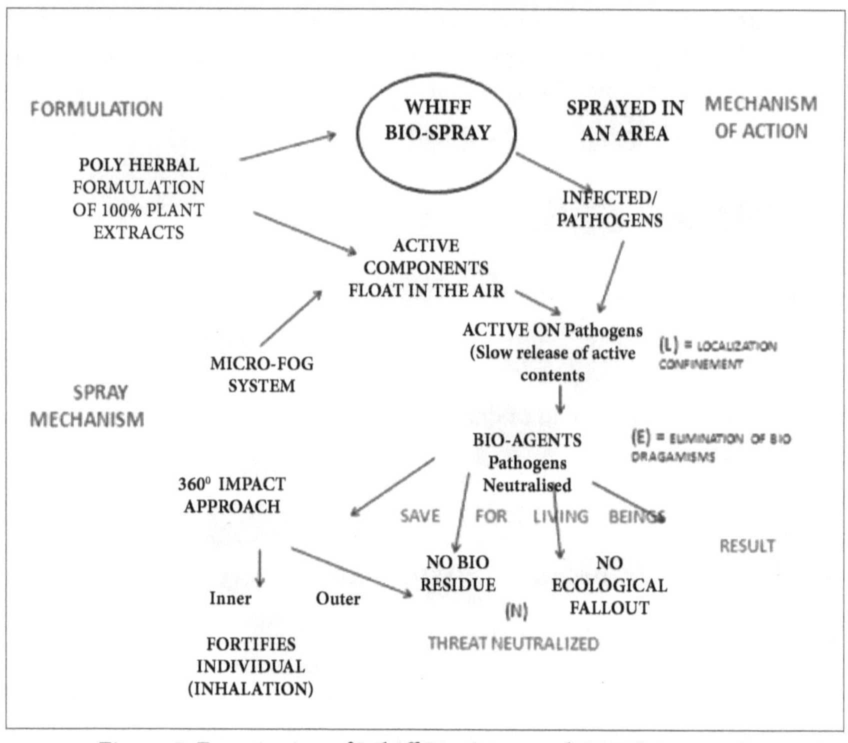

Figure 5: Functioning of Whiff Bio-Spray and QLEN Approach

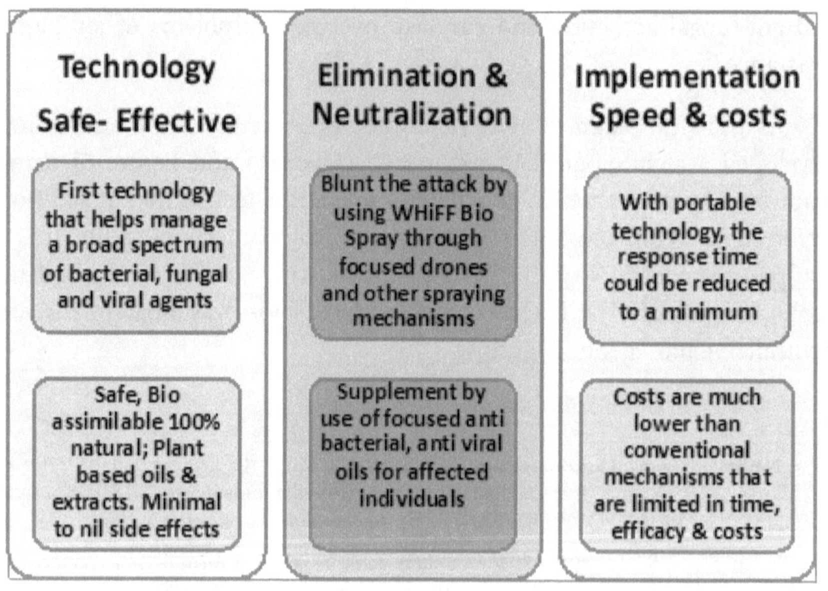

Figure 6: Whiff Bio-Spray features and benefits

Effectiveness of Whiff Bio-Spray

Efficacy of the Whiff Bio-Spray was tested upon different drug resistant pathogens with varying concentrations of the plant extract actives. The efficacy was tested both in a laboratory environment and in a real-life situation.

The tests on bio-agents were done through the Four Plate test to map efficacy and anti-microbial action of the Whiff Bio-Spray on the air microbes. The bio-spray was further tested on total bacterial, yeast and mould count, E. Coli, Salmonella, Pseudomonas aeruginosa and Staphylococcus aureus. Viable bio-organisms were reported before bio-spray, and four hours after bio-spray in 12x8 ft room. A notable reduction was measured in bio-organisms by 68 to 93 percent after bio-spray in the controlled laboratory room (Table 1). A higher concentrate Whiff bio-spray countered the pathogen count to completely eliminate them, as was seen in the pilot study conducted at All India Institute of Medical Science (AIIMS) Delhi. Microbial count was also significantly countered by the Whiff Bio-Spray (Table 2).

Table 1: Bacteria Pathogen Plate Test in Laboratory (Report No. DTRLF-100118080) conducted at a National Accreditation Board of Testing and Calibration of Laboratories

Description	Microbial examination in 12x8' room (in colony forming unit [cfu])		Percentage reduction in Microbes after the bio-spray
	Before Spray	After Spray	
Plate1 in LAF	18	2	88.88
Plate2 in LAF Floor	25	8	68.00
Plate3 in Sterility Section Gate	23	5	78.26
Plate4 in Sterility Mid-Point	15	1	93.33

Table 2: Microbial contamination test in the laboratory (Report No. DTRLF-100118076) conducted at a NABL certified laboratory

Microbial Test for	Result
Total bacterial count	Less than 10 cfu/ml
Total yeast and mould count	Less than 10 cfu/ml
E. Coli	Absent in 1 ml
Salmonella	Absent in 10 ml
Pseudomonas aeruginosa	Absent in 1ml
Staphylococcus aureus	Absent in 1ml

After the laboratory test, bio-spray effectiveness pilot study was conducted in real-life set up in a controlled hospital environment in accordance with the protocol of the hospital at the Department of Microbiology of AIIMS, Delhi. The results have shown a significant reduction of air-pathogens. This indicates that the bio-spray is effective to counter bio-agents in the air and in turn will protect from the ill effects of it.

Discussion

Barton Gellman, an American journalist, has indicated that "in biological weapons there is almost no prospect of detecting a pathogen until it has been used in an attack". Considering the same, Whiff Bio-Spray is an effective tool (Figure 7) to counter a fatal attack due to unknown bio-agents. Following the QLEN model, Whiff bio-spray will be able to counter the air-borne spread of bio-organisms quickly irrespective of the geographical area, wherever required. Thus, Whiff Bio-Spray is an effective decontamination measure. Decontamination means to remove or neutralize chemical and biological weapons (CBW) to limit their exposure to humans[18] and at present there is no direct solution to neutralize and eliminate these bio-organisms (bio-weapons). Under biodefense against bio attack, medical measures are suggested to protect people, viz. medicines and vaccinations; and other preventive measures like non-exposure to air.[19] These measures work on the after-effects of bio-attack rather than on the exact payload of bio-attack (that is bio-organisms) where Whiff bio-spray is the effective bio-assimilable natural herbal solution. Further, a study indicates that

18 White, S. M. *op. cit.*

19 https://medlineplus.gov/biodefenseandbioterrorism.html#cat_59. *op. cit.*

plant-based essential oils are effective to deal with the problem of antibiotic resistance.[20] Again, Whiff Bio-Spray will be able to counter the antibiotic resistant bio-agents.

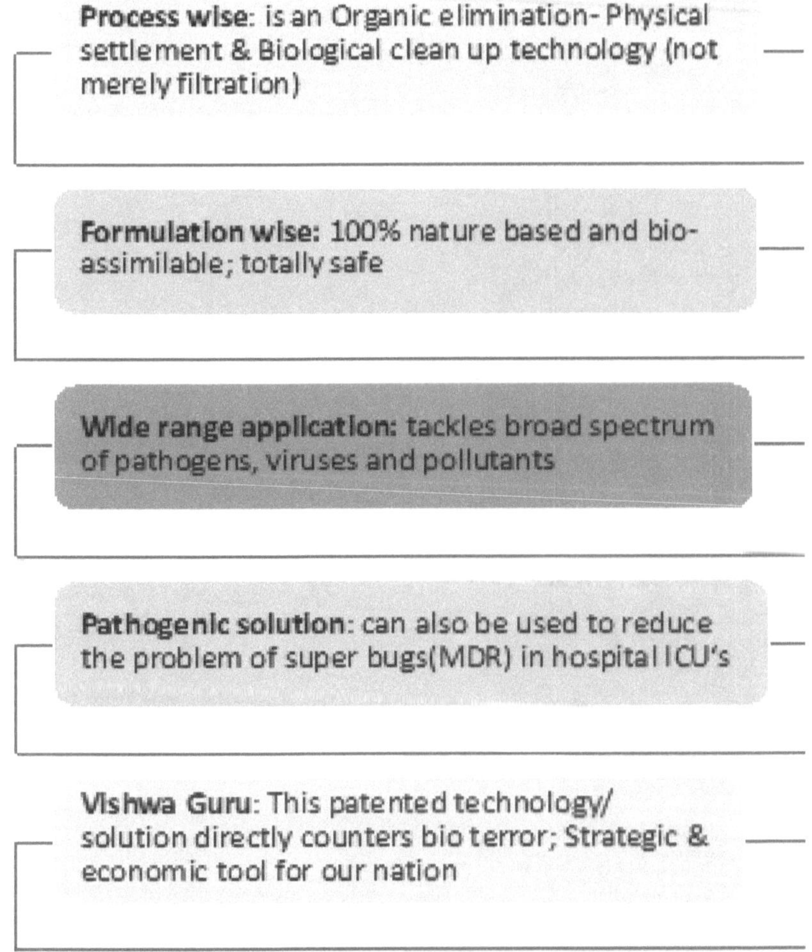

Figure 7: Whiff Bio-Spray: a unique inventio

Conclusion

The invention of Whiff Bio-Spray to counter and neutralise pathogenic bio-agents directly by eliminating them from the area of attack, whether towards naturally occurring diseases or deliberate bio-attack, is an

---

20 Priti, V. *op. cit.*

effective primary measure to counter a bio-terror attack. Whiff Bio-Spray is 100 percent plant extract-based solution and bio-assimilable with no side-effects. Knowledge, access and usage of Whiff Bio-Spray can help individuals, communities and nations to fight bio-threats both safely and economically.

14

Challenges to the Region from Transnational Terrorism

Mr. Hekmatullah Azamy

There is a need to decode the relationship between the various terror groups that are operating in the region, like the Taliban, Al Qaeda, Islamic State (IS), Islamic Movement of Uzbekistan (IMU), etc and see if they can work together. There is also a need to understand what is preventing these groups from working together. In fact, it has emerged that Taliban and IS are the main rivals. Al Qaeda was an old associate of Taliban but same cannot be confirmed now. There are three main groups that have emerged, Taliban, IS and Al Qaeda that are fighting to maintain influence. Taliban and IS are competing for control of territory but Al Qaeda is more focused to maintain cognitive influence. The IMU is divided; one faction is siding and supporting IS, other is with the Taliban and Al Qaida nexus. East Turkistan Islamic movement (ETIM) the largest group of Uighurs fighters and has approximately 1000 plus fighters that are now located in Afghanistan. ETIM is also split, with one supporting IS while the other is supporting Taliban/Al Qaeda nexus.

The situation is of course, complex in Afghanistan. Overall assessment is that when the foreign or international terrorists are given a free choice to choose between Taliban and groups such as Al Qaeda or Daesh then often their choice is going to be either Daesh or Al Qaeda due to similarity in ideology, meanwhile; the senior leadership also does not allow the involvement of foreign terrorist.

Taliban, however, at a local level does seek support. Hence, it is not a nationalistic group, rather it has transnational elements. The first element is that this pattern might have existed previously and might exist in the future as well. In 2017, Asim Umar, head of AQIS (Al Qaeda in the Indian Subcontinent) covertly supported Daesh. The reason behind doing so is to open a new front with Taliban. ETIM Abdul Haq, who turned out to be in alliance, in his speeches claimed that groups such as IMU switching to Taliban is a mistake as it only encourages internal fights, distracting from fighting the common goal.

The second element that needs to be understood is that the return of the people who had left from Afghanistan for Iraq and Syria, can be important, to predict the future pattern of groups in the regions. When Zarb-e-arz became operational in 2014, many people have shifted either to Afghanistan or further to Iraq and Syria. While the Arab terrorists made the shift with their entire families, Central Asians have left them behind with an intention to return. These elements are now returning along with terrorists from Russia and Europe making Afghanistan a centre of terrorist activity.

Such trends should be monitored to make good assessments. One other such scenario is the silence of Daesh. Silence from Daesh or Al Qaeda should not be translated to a victory. Rather, they should still be considered as a serious threat to security.

Now, the question is what needs to be done? Firstly, it is important to understand that it is extremely difficult to fight these terrorists until and unless one understands them correctly. A critical evaluation should be made of our understanding.

Country's intelligence agencies that can be expected to have a proper understanding of what these groups are up to, do not have necessary information. Hence, for a country like India, which has been a long-standing strategic partner of Afghanistan, the situation at ground level needs to be understood before engaging in any capacity. Secondly, it can be observed that countries that might be rivals or have divergent interests on global levels, have a similar interest when it comes to Afghanistan. For example, even though China and India might not be at the same level on issues of borders, economics and trade, it is in interest of both the countries that Afghanistan remains peaceful. Thus, it is essential to exploit such an opportunity.

15

Technology as an Enabler to deal with Transnational Terrorism

Ms. Aadya Shukla

Technologies like the AI can be used to address the problem of transnational terrorism. The first focus should be at identifying issues related to the same so that a sustainable implementation can be provided. The next area of focus should be to talk about components at different layers of cyber space, which would provide sustainable deployment of technology. Systematic thinking is the most important element in applying technology to tackle the transnational terrorism. AI can help us in cyber physical, logical, application, societal and dominance layer. Maritime security at cyber layer and application layers are widely addressed. Hence, it is required that all the ideas are placed in a systematic way to achieve the desired goals.

AI is often referred to as technology. However, in an alternate view, AI can be considered as a paradigm. It is a way of thinking. Hence, it is important to focus on the previously mentioned five core layers. AI can help in development centred on defence and military. At the top layer, it would seem that there have been admirable efforts. However, AI sufficiency is more or less fragmented. Building AI sufficiency should be concentrated on. One way of doing so is by looking at the security at hardware level. Concentrated effort on development of cyber capabilities is another way.

The next point is related to supply chain management, interoperability challenge and the AI side of capacity building, public private participation. One important aspect to look at is the information related to security matters, like a potential terrorist attack requires going through various channels and delaying action. To tackle this situation private-public partnerships should be considered, similar to what Western countries like the U.S. and UK are adopting.

AI is Important - However, to use AI the most salient requirement is that of customised hardware. So, for example as far as hardware is concerned, AI heavily relies on processing the CPU, even the fastest and most advanced CPU, may not improve the speed of training in AI model. AI is of six different kinds. These differentiations are closely related to the financial availability for the nation. So, while making a decision at policy level, what to define and what not to define, awareness of themes is essential. We should be aware of what would fulfil our future needs. Currently, there are various manufacturers such as Intel that will help in achieving the set goals. The focus, hence, should be on funding of those goals, then on procurement and supply chain investment. Another thing which is very important is the convergence of AI and IOT, especially as AI and IOT are at the edge of company layers. So, most of the models are actually going to be deployed in the public cloud. Hence, the focus should be on the Application layer where most of the convergence of AI and IOT happens. Market forces drive the development offer. While discussing the use of AI, the most symbolic should be the line and the type of machine learning. Looking at India, it can be observed that there are developers in the field, but not any innovators and designers. This requires collaborations from other nations. These collaborations can prove advantageous for India.

India should monitor the developing technologies and progress in the field. There should be collaboration with different stakeholders from domains of academia and policy making. When it comes to technology, a country like India cannot afford to be out-dated. AI sufficiency is, hence, need of the hour. Technologies are already there along with innovations. Provisions to exchange technologies can be put into place as sustained sufficiency has no alternative.

16

International Cooperation against Terror Funding: A Potent Tool to Combat Terrorism

Maj Gen IM Yusuf

It has been widely acknowledged, that money is the lifeblood of terrorism and thus, if one dries up the sources of terror that is their blood supply, the terrorist will gradually become weak and eventually die. Many scholars of terrorism have continued to advocate for the need to 'follow the money' in order to identify and track the diverse networks involved in terrorism financing.[1] Tracing networks responsible for terror financing was not too difficult during the Cold War era because nation states were the predominant actors in sponsorship of terrorism. However, in the aftermath of the Cold War, there was an emergence of non-state terrorist groups who began to diversify their sources of funding, as state sponsorship declined substantially. Additionally, this era has become characterised by a number of failing and failed states which has created conducive environment for the growth of insurgent and/or terrorist organisations especially in ungoverned spaces in some parts of Africa and Asia.[2] Also, globalisation and the emergence of new technologies have made it easier to move money across international borders. While efforts have been made to contain and suppress the terror financing both at national and international levels, it

---

1   Kyari, M. (2019) "Boko Haram Threats and the Challenges of Nigeria's Counter Insurgency Strategy" being a lecture delivered at the Defence Intelligence College, Abuja, Nigeria on 13 August 2019.

2   Jean K, Giraldo. and H.A. Trinkunas (2007). Terrorism Financing and State Responses: A Comparative Perspective, California: Stanford University Press. pp.10

was only after 11 September 2001 (9/11) that significant milestones were achieved in the international collaboration against terrorism financing, with USA and EU taking the lead. However, their focus then was mainly on Al Qaeda and the Taliban wherever, they were based. Several terrorist groups which were not in the U.S. terror list have continued to thrive with little or no tracking as to their source of funding, networking and violent activities.

Theoretically, countering terrorism financing involves a classic collective action approach. There has been a rapid adoption of international conventions on countering terrorism financing, especially in the wake of the September 11, 2001 attacks on the U.S. However, limited success has been achieved in the implementation of these conventions, largely because nation states adopt these legislations to avoid the penalties of non-adherence. Moreover, many states lack the institutional capacity to successfully enforce the counter terrorism financing (CTF) norms and practices due to the informal nature of their economies.

This paper has argued that the current international efforts to strangle terrorism financing are largely superficial, due to the conflicting interests of the U.S. on one hand and other major players such as the EU on the other. This paper begins with a clarification of the concept of terrorism financing and provides a broad categorization of sources of terrorism funding. It has identified the major international legal frameworks against terrorism financing and has given a synopsis of international efforts at curbing the menace. Finally, the paper offers some recommendations that would enhance current efforts in suppressing terrorist financing.

Conceptual Clarification

A comprehensive definition is offered by the International Convention for the Suppression of Terrorism Financing.[3] It defines funds for terrorism as:

> "Assets of every kind, whether tangible or intangible, movable or immovable, however acquired, and legal documents or instruments in any form, including electronic or digital, evidencing title to, or interest in, such assets, including, but not limited to, bank credits, travellers' cheques, bank cheques, money orders, shares, securities, bonds, drafts and letters of credit."

---

3 United Nations (1999) International Convention for the Suppression of the Financing of Terrorism.

Going further, it sets out terrorism financing to be a situation whereby, a person "by any means, directly or indirectly, unlawfully and wilfully, provides or collects funds with the intention that they should be used or in the knowledge that they are to be used, in full or in part, in order to carry out an act of terrorism". It is vital to note that it is the intention that such funds be used, or the knowledge (whether full or partial) that are to be used for terrorism that matters. The definition encompasses the act of attempting to participate, organise, contribute or directing the provision or collection of such funds. However, it is not necessary for the funds to be actually used to commit an offence.[4] Put differently, for the crime of terrorism financing to take place, the establishment of a '*mens rea*' will be sufficient; an intention is what is necessary.

Major Sources of Terrorism Funding

The sources of terrorism financing are quite diverse (formal and informal financial sources) and have continued to evolve with emerging technologies, globalization, transnational organized crimes, proliferation of charitable organisations and the complex nature of the informal financial sector of some national economies, amongst others. It is also worth noting that each terrorist organisation utilizes a combination of sources depending on the peculiar context of its operating environment. A good understanding of how terrorists raise, move, store and use money will assist national and international efforts in suppressing their funding means and methods. Achi and Tar[5] have placed these sources into 5 broad categories which are as follows:

(a) State sponsorship in the form of proxy war.

(b) Organised crimes – kidnapping, drugs, arms and human trafficking, smuggling, cattle rustling, money laundering, piracy, robbery, etc.

(c) Donations - sympathetic individuals and groups, '*hawala*'.

(d) Entrepreneurial ventures - usually legitimate businesses.

(c) Cyber related crimes - online money laundering, identity and credit card theft etc.

---

4   Ibid, pp.2-3

5   Achi, NK and Tar, U.A (2013) Understanding the Financing of Terrorism: Conceptual and Empirical Notes. *Journal of Defence Studies*, Volume 18 (March): pp 171 190

A careful study of the sources of funding would lead to some deductions. First, in conflict zones such as the Lake Chad Basin, there has been a strong direct nexus between organized crimes and financing of terrorism. Second, terrorist groups such as Boko Haram have relied on multiple sources of funding and the bulk of illicit activities take place in the informal financial sector. Third, ungoverned spaces within the region provide a good atmosphere for illicit enterprises that finance Boko Haram. Finally, there are a substantial number of persons within the region which have donated money to terrorist groups without knowing so. Having identified these diverse and complex sources of funding, a fundamental question arises. How can the International community respond effectively to terrorism financing?

International Legal Frameworks

International financial regulatory frameworks and controls are vital to countering terrorism, because 'money is the lifeblood of terrorism' hence, preventing and countering threats of terrorism has remained a top priority for the international community despite the divergent perspectives of some states. Since 1963, the international community has activated nineteen international legal instruments to prevent terrorist acts.[6] Prominent amongst these frameworks is the 1999 International Convention for the Suppression of the Financing of terrorism that directly deals with countering terror financing. The Convention requires parties to take steps to prevent and counteract the financing of terrorists, whether direct or indirect, through groups, claiming to have charitable, social or cultural goals or which also engage in illicit activities such as drug trafficking or gun running. It has also committed states to hold those who finance terrorism, criminally, civilly or administratively, liable for such acts and provides for the identification, freezing and seizure of funds allocated for terrorist activities, as well as for the sharing of the forfeited funds with other States on a case-by-case basis.[7] Similarly, the UN Security Council (UNSC) Resolution 1269 of 1999, specifically called on all countries "to prevent and suppress the preparation and financing of terrorist acts

---

6 UNDOC (2009) National Workshop on the Universal Legal Framework Against Terrorism held at Funa Futi, Tuualu, 24 - 27 April 2009, www.unodc.org/documents/ southeastasiaandpacific/2009/05/Universal-Legal -Framework-against-Terrorism-Workshop/1_General.pdf.

7 Ibid

through all possible legal means".[8] This was the first UNSC resolution to address terrorism financing.

In the aftermath of the events of 11 September 2001, the UNSC had adopted Resolution 1373[9] which has required all states to prevent and suppress the financing of terrorist acts and to refrain from providing support to those involved in them. It has also established the Security Council's Counter Terrorism Committee (CTC) to monitor state compliance with its provisions. Since the adoption of this resolution, the rate of adherence has increased significantly. For instance, two thirds of the UN member states have ratified or acceded to at least 10 out of the 19 instruments and there is no longer any country that has neither signed nor become a party to at least one of them.[10] While these Resolutions have clearly demonstrated the desire by the international community to tackle financing of terrorism, each of them have focused on specific acts of terrorism because member states are unwilling to uniformly define terrorism and terrorists.[11] Thus, the lack of political will by some member states and the inability of the UN to enforce compliance amongst other challenges have limited the attainment of the objectives of these regulations.

International Efforts to Combat Terrorist Financing

The international community has continued to expend a lot of efforts and resources to combat the threats of terrorism in general. The efforts of the international community to combat terrorist financing has been discussed in second segments - Pre 9/11 and Post 9/11 eras. These two eras have been presented side by side, because the end of the Cold War was perhaps the most trail blazing moment for the blossoming of terrorist and insurgent groups. This was the result of the failure of the state, after the Cold War, to control or contain terrorist groups. As during the Cold War era many states were deeply involved in the game of terror funding.

---

8   UNSCR 1269 (1999) Adopted by the Security Council at its 4053rd meeting, on 19 October 1999, (http://unscr.com/files/1999/01269.pdf)

9   UNSCR 1373 (2001)   Adopted by the Security Council at its 4385[th]Meeting, 28 September (www.unodc.org/pdf/crime/terrorism/rcs_1373_english.pdf).

10 UNSCR 2462 (2019) Adopted at the UNSC 8496th Meeting on 28 March 2019, unscr. com/en/resolutions/doc/2462.

11 Clunan, A.L. (2007) "U.S. and International Responses to Terrorist Financing", in: Jeanne, K. (eds) *Terrorism Financing and State Responses*, California: Standford University Press, pp. 263.

Pre 9/11 Era

Prior to 9/11 the main effort of the International Community was on countering state sponsorship of terrorism. This disposition changed following the bombing of the U.S. embassies in Tanzania and Kenya. After these incidences, the searchlight was extended to cover activities such as money laundering and criminal finance by non-state actors such as Hamas and Hezbollah.[12] Pressure in the form of sanctions was brought to bear on states such as Libya and Sudan to desist from sponsorship of terrorism. Consequently, the 1999 UN Convention for the Suppression of Financing Terrorism categorically stated the responsibilities of nation states regarding the actions of non-state actors within their jurisdictions. Additionally, the Financial Action Task Force (FATF) on Money Laundering was created to tackle the problem of organized criminal finance. In 2000, the FATF initiated a campaign of 'naming and shaming' countries that violated best practices in combating transnational financial crimes. This has encouraged many countries to domesticate these legislations and deter money laundering. At the national level, a network of Financial Intelligence Units (FIUs) were created to serve as a forum for sharing information on money laundering across national frontiers, as well as providing capacity building of national staff, to deal with money laundering related matters.

Post 9/11 Era

In the Post 9/11 period, the U.S. had taken the lead in harnessing the international efforts in combating terrorism financing and other terrorist acts, largely because of the direct impact of the terrorist attack of September 2011 on its national survival and interests as a nation. It was therefore, not surprising that the U.S. had become the main sponsor of most of the UNSC resolutions on terrorist acts. However, the U.S. appears to prefer bilateral and regional frameworks to monitor and encourage compliance rather than focusing on global multinational regime. For instance, in 2004, out of the $2.2 million given to the UN to implement technical assistance in CTF, the USA contributed less than 10 percent while Austria alone made up over half.[13] The U.S. views the multilateral approach as a 'waste of time'. This perspective may not be unconnected, as with complex bureaucracy it is difficult to get a consensus when working along a multilateral

---

12 Ibid

13 Ibid, pp.267

approach, in view of the divergent interests of nation states. Although U.S. supports the work of the UN, it prefers targeting Islamist groups rather than combating terrorism more generally.[14] On the contrary, the EU and other major actors within the international system tend to prefer a global multi-lateral approach designed to address the root causes of terrorism, including rule of law through the UN system. It is not unlikely that the U.S. approach is influenced by its desire to avoid the huge financial costs involved in addressing the root causes of terrorism, as this will involve broader developmental issues.

From the foregoing, it is not unreasonable to conclude that International efforts on suppressing terrorism financing appear to be superficial, largely due to the divergent approaches adopted by the major players. Most effective cooperation takes place at bilateral levels, largely because of conflicting interests of nation states. Additionally, the bulk of the efforts of the international community tend to focus on the traditional formal sectors of the economy, largely because of the obsession with major terrorist organisations, while little or no attention has been given to terrorist organisations at sub-regional or regional levels operating predominantly, in the informal financial sector.

Way Forward to Combating Terrorists Financing

(a) Address the root causes of terrorism and the conditions that make it easier for terrorist financing and other criminal activities to thrive like governance deficit, corruption, injustice etc.

(b) Nation states need to adopt a flexible, comprehensive and multidimensional approach to combating terrorism financing at national and regional levels in order to dry up the diverse sources of funds being exploited by terrorists.

(c) Embark on an extensive and sustained sensitization campaigns to educate citizens on sources of terrorist funds and how to stifle them.

(d) Strengthen legal frameworks including criminal justice system, to effectively tackle organized crimes both within and across national boundaries. In view of the nexus between organized crimes and

---

14 Ibid

terrorism, all states must develop robust legal frameworks, to criminalize the financing of terrorism.

(e) Enforce laws, collect and share real-time intelligence and documentary evidence, use financial intelligence experts and criminal investigators, prosecutors, custom agents, bank employees as well as 'Bureau de Change' operators.

(f) Build national institutional capacity to combat terrorism financing, because it is a crime that requires specially trained financial experts to track the movement of funds.

Conclusion

This paper has revealed the nature and scope of terrorism financing and notes that in spite of the bilateral and multilateral efforts to track and contain terror financing, there has been limited success due to disparate interests and commitments of the cooperating countries. In addition, it has revealed that terrorism financing has evolved differently during and after the Cold War era. Terrorists have continued to raise and move funds for their activities and exploited governance deficits, the weaknesses of state financial institutions and the informal nature of economies especially, in parts of Africa and Asia. This paper has offered a number of recommendations – which include the strengthening of municipal and international institutions and strategies, and the involvement of both state and non-state actors, to deny terrorist and insurgent groups the vital financial oxygen that they need to survive and perpetuate their violent activities. Unless terrorism financing is eliminated, it would be difficult to contain or defeat terrorism across the world.